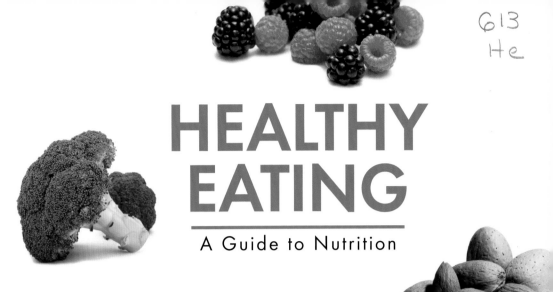

HEALTHY EATING

A Guide to Nutrition

Basic Nutrition

Second Edition

HEALTHY EATING: A GUIDE TO NUTRITION

Basic Nutrition, Second Edition

Nutrition and Disease Prevention

Nutrition and Eating Disorders, Second Edition

Nutrition and Food Safety

Nutrition and Weight Management, Second Edition

Nutrition for Sports and Exercise, Second Edition

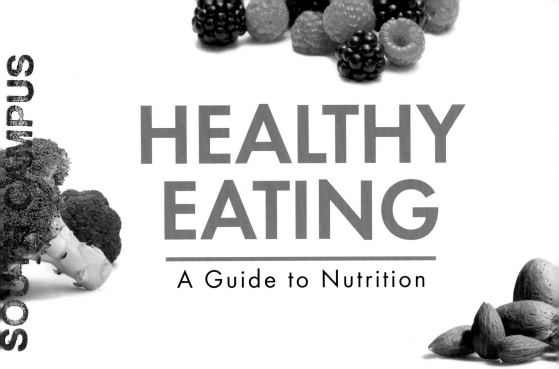

HEALTHY EATING

A Guide to Nutrition

Basic Nutrition
Second Edition

Lori A. Smolin, Ph.D., and
Mary B. Grosvenor, M.S., R.D.

CHELSEA HOUSE
PUBLISHERS
An imprint of Infobase Publishing

Chelsea House
An imprint of Infobase Publishing
132 West 31st Street
New York, NY 10001

Library of Congress Cataloging-in-Publication Data
Smolin, Lori A.
 Basic nutrition / Lori A. Smolin and Mary B. Grosvenor. — 2nd ed.
  p. cm. — (Healthy eating: A guide to nutrition)
 Includes bibliographical references and index.
 ISBN 978-1-60413-801-6 (hardcover)
 1. Nutrition. I. Grosvenor, Mary B. II. Title. III. Series.
 QP141.S5373 2010
 612.3—dc22   2010005696

Chelsea House books are available at special discounts when purchased in bulk quantities for businesses, associations, institutions, or sales promotions. Please call our Special Sales Department in New York at (212) 967-8800 or (800) 322-8755.

You can find Chelsea House on the World Wide Web at
http://www.chelseahouse.com.

Text design by Annie O'Donnell
Cover design by Alicia Post
Illustrations by Sholto Ainslie for Infobase Publishing
Composition by Mary Susan Ryan-Flynn
Cover printed by Bang Printing, Brainerd, Minn.
Book printed and bound by Bang Printing, Brainerd, Minn.
Date printed: October 2010
Printed in the United States of America

10 9 8 7 6 5 4 3 2 1

This book is printed on acid-free paper.

All links and web addresses were checked and verified to be correct at the time of publication. Because of the dynamic nature of the web, some addresses and links may have changed since publication and may no longer be valid.

CONTENTS

Introduction   7
by Lori A. Smolin, Ph.D., and
Mary B. Grosvenor, M.S., R.D.

1 What Is Nutrition?   9

2 Carbohydrates   29

3 Dietary Fiber   48

4 Lipids   60

5 Protein   78

6 Water   94

7 Vitamins   111

8 Minerals   139

9 Choosing a Healthy Diet   166

Appendices
  Dietary Reference Intakes   *181*
  Healthy Body Weight   *188*
  Blood Values of Nutritional Relevance   *192*
  USDA's MyPyramid   *193*

Glossary   194

Bibliography   210

Further Resources   215

Picture Credits   217

Index   218

About the Authors   224

INTRODUCTION

A hundred years ago, people received nutritional guidance from mothers and grandmothers: Eat your carrots because they're good for your eyes; don't eat too many potatoes because they'll make you fat; be sure to get plenty of roughage so you can more easily move your bowels. Today, everyone seems to offer more advice: Take a vitamin supplement to optimize your health; don't eat fish with cabbage because you won't be able to digest them together; you can't stay healthy on a vegetarian diet. Nutrition is one of those topics about which all people seem to think they know something, or at least have an opinion. Whether it is the clerk in your local health food store recommending that you buy supplements or the woman behind you in line at the grocery store raving about the latest low-carbohydrate diet, everyone is ready to offer you nutritional advice. How do you know what to believe or, more importantly, what to do?

The purpose of these books is to help you answer these questions. Even if you don't love learning about science, at the very least you probably enjoy certain foods and want to stay healthy—or become healthier. In response to this, these books are designed to make the science you *need* to understand as palatable as the foods you love. Once you understand the basics, you can apply this simple health knowledge to your everyday decisions about nutrition and health. The **Healthy Eating** set includes one book with all of the basic nutrition information you need to choose a healthy diet, as well as five others that cover topics of special concern to many: weight management, exercise, disease prevention, food safety, and eating disorders.

Our goal is not to tell you to stop eating potato chips and candy bars, give up fast food, or always eat your vegetables. Instead, it is to provide you with the information you need to make informed choices about your diet. We hope you will recognize that potato chips and candy are not poison, but they should only be eaten as occasional treats. We hope you will decide for yourself that fast food is something you can indulge in every now and then, but is not a good choice every day. We encourage you to recognize that although you should eat your vegetables, not everyone always does, so you should do your best to try new vegetables and fruits and eat them as often as possible.

These books take the science of nutrition out of the classroom and allow you to apply this information to the choices you make about foods, exercise, dietary supplements, and other lifestyle decisions that are important to your health. This knowledge should help you choose a healthy diet while allowing you to enjoy the diversity of flavors, textures, and tastes that food provides, and also encouraging you to explore the meanings food holds in our society. When you eat a healthy diet, you will feel good in the short term and enjoy health benefits in the long term. We can't personally evaluate each meal you consume, but we believe these books will give you the tools to make your own nutritious choices.

Lori A. Smolin, Ph.D., and
Mary B. Grosvenor, M.S., R.D.

1

WHAT IS NUTRITION?

Nutrition is the study of all of the interactions that occur between people and the food they eat. It involves understanding which nutrients the human body needs, what kind of foods contain them, how the human body uses them, and the impact they have on human health. Nutrition also involves sociological, cultural, economic, and technological factors and the role they play in obtaining and choosing the foods we eat.

WE GET NUTRIENTS FROM FOOD

Humans don't eat individual **nutrients**; they eat food. Food provides the body with energy and nutrients; it also contains other substances, such as chemicals found in plants. These chemicals are called **phytochemicals**. Although they have not been defined as nutrients, they do have health-promoting properties.

When we eat the right combination of foods, our diet provides all of the nutrients and other substances we need to stay healthy. If we choose a poor combination of foods, we may be missing out on some nutrients and consuming others in excess.

There are more than 40 nutrients that are essential to human life. We need to consume these **essential nutrients** in our diets because our bodies either cannot make them or they cannot make them in large enough amounts for optimal health. Different foods contain different nutrients in varying amounts and combinations. For example, beef, chicken, and fish provide protein, vitamin B_6, and iron; bread, rice, and pastas provide carbohydrate, folic acid, and niacin; fruits and vegetables provide carbohydrate, fiber, vitamin A, and vitamin C; and vegetable oils provide fat and vitamin E. In addition to the nutrients that they naturally contain, many foods have nutrients added to them by **fortification** to replace losses that occur during cooking and processing or to supplement the diet. Dietary supplements are also a source of nutrients. Although most people can meet their nutrient needs without them, supplements can be useful for maintaining health and preventing deficiencies.

Choosing a diet that provides enough of all the essential nutrients without excesses of calories or nutrients can be a challenge because we eat for many reasons other than to obtain nutrients. We eat because we enjoy the sight or smell of certain foods, it's lunchtime, we're at a party, we're in a sad or a happy mood, it's a holiday, and a multitude of other reasons. In order to meet nutrient needs, we must understand what these needs are and how to choose a diet that provides them.

WHAT DO NUTRIENTS DO?

Nutrients provide three basic functions for the body. Some nutrients provide energy, some provide structure, and some help to regulate the processes that keep us alive. Each nutrient performs one or more of these functions, and all nutrients together are needed for growth, for maintenance and repair, and for reproduction.

Energy

Nutrients provide the body with the energy or fuel it needs to stay alive, to move, and to grow. This energy keeps the heart pumping, the lungs respiring, and the body warm. It is also used to keep the stomach churning and the muscles working. Carbohydrates, **lipids,** and proteins are the only nutrients that provide energy to the body; they are referred to as the **energy-yielding nutrients.** The energy used by the body is measured in **calories** or **kilocalories** (abbreviated as "kcalories" or "kcals"). In some other countries, food energy is measured in joules or **kilojoules** (abbreviated as "kjoules" or "kJs").

Each gram of carbohydrate provides the body with 4 calories. A gram of protein also provides 4 calories; a gram of fat provides 9 calories, more than twice the calories of carbohydrates or protein. For this reason, foods that are high in fat are high in calories. Alcohol can also provide energy in the diet, 7 calories per gram, but alcohol is not considered a nutrient because the body does not need it for survival.

The more calories a person uses, the more calories need to be supplied in the diet to maintain weight. Increasing exercise without

IS A CALORIE A KILOCALORIE?

There are 16 calories in a teaspoon of sugar. Yet, if in your chemistry class you measured the amount of energy in a teaspoon of sugar, the result would be about 16,000 calories, or 16 kilocalories. This is because the "calories" we use in nutrition to refer to the energy content of food are really kilocalories. A kilocalorie is 1,000 calories. Sometimes, as is the case on food labels, *calorie* is spelled with a capital "C" to indicate that it is referring to kilocalories. In the popular press, however, the term *calorie* with a lower case "c" is typically used to express the kilocalorie content of a food or of a diet. Therefore, when you eat a cookie that has 50 calories, keep in mind that it really has 50 kilocalories, or 50,000 calories.

increasing the amount of food eaten will lead to weight loss. Increasing food intake without increasing exercise will cause the extra energy to be stored, mostly as fat, resulting in weight gain. When a person consumes the same number of calories as he or she uses, body weight remains the same—this means the person is in **energy balance**.

Structure

There is truth to the saying "you are what you eat" because all of the structures in our bodies are formed from the nutrients we consume in our diet. By weight, our bodies are about 60% water, 16% protein, 16% fat, and 6% minerals. Water is a structural nutrient because it plumps up the **cells**, giving them their shape. Protein forms the structure of tendons, ligaments, and muscles and lipids are the major component of body fat; muscle and fat give the body its shape. The minerals calcium and phosphorus harden the bones, which provide the structural frame of the body and determine one's height and the length of the arms and legs.

Regulation

Nutrients are also important regulators of body functions. All of the processes that occur in our bodies, from the breakdown of carbohydrates and fat to provide energy, to the building of bone and muscle to form body structures, must be regulated for the body to function normally. For instance, the chemical reactions that maintain body temperature at 98.6°F (37°C) must be regulated or body temperature will rise above or fall below the healthy range. This constant internal body environment is called **homeostasis**. Maintaining homeostasis requires many different nutrients. Carbohydrates help to label proteins that must be removed from the blood. Water helps to regulate body temperature. Lipids and proteins are needed to make regulatory **molecules** called **hormones**, and certain protein molecules, **vitamins**, and minerals help to regulate the rate of chemical reactions within the body.

GETTING NUTRIENTS TO YOUR CELLS

To get nutrients to the cells that need them, food must be digested and its nutrients must be absorbed. **Digestion** breaks food into small molecules and **absorption** brings these substances into the body, where they are transported to the cells.

The digestive system is responsible for the digestion and absorption of food (Figure 1.1). The main part of this system is the **gastrointestinal tract,** also called the GI tract. The GI tract is a hollow tube that starts at the mouth. From there food passes down the **esophagus** into the stomach and then on into the small intestine. Rhythmic contractions of the smooth muscles lining the GI tract help mix the food and propel it along. Substances, such as **mucus** and **enzymes**, are secreted into the GI tract to help with the movement and digestion of food. The digestive system also secretes hormones into the blood that help regulate GI activity. Most of the digestion and absorption of nutrients occurs in the small intestine. Once absorbed, nutrients are transported in the blood to the cells. Any material that has not been absorbed passes into the large intestine. Here, water and small amounts of some nutrients can be absorbed and the remaining wastes are excreted in the **feces.**

HOW THE BODY USES NUTRIENTS

Once they are inside body cells, carbohydrates, lipids, and proteins are involved in chemical reactions; the sum of these chemical reactions that occur inside body cells is called **metabolism**. The chemical reactions of metabolism synthesize the molecules needed to form body structures such as muscles, nerves, and bones. The reactions of metabolism also break down carbohydrates, lipids, and proteins to yield energy in the form of **adenosine triphosphate (ATP)**. ATP is a molecule that is used by cells as an energy source to do work such as pumping blood, contracting muscles, or synthesizing new body tissue.

Digestive System

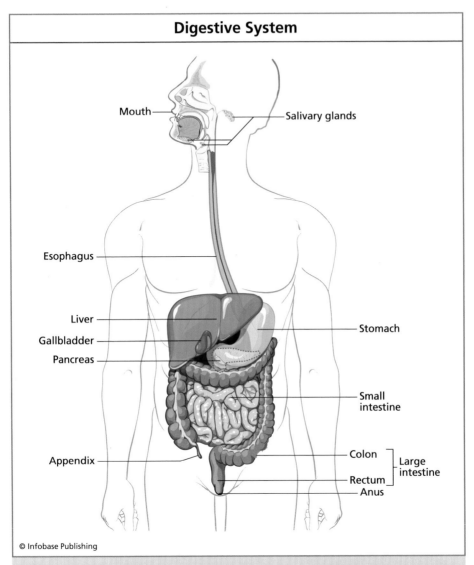

Mouth

Salivary glands

Esophagus

Liver

Stomach

Gallbladder

Pancreas

Small intestine

Appendix

Colon ⌉
Large intestine

Rectum ⌋

Anus

FIGURE 1.1 The digestive system consists of the gastrointestinal tract (mouth, esophagus, stomach, small intestine, and large intestine) and accessory organs that secrete substances that aid digestion and absorption (salivary glands, liver, and pancreas). Beginning with the first bite, the digestive system starts the process of breaking down foods into units that are small enough to be absorbed into the body.

THE SIX CLASSES OF NUTRIENTS

The nutrients we need come from six different classes: carbohydrates, lipids, proteins, water, vitamins, and minerals. Each of these classes, with the exception of water, includes a variety of different molecules that are used by the body in different ways (Table 1.1). Carbohydrates, lipids, proteins, and water are often referred to as **macronutrients** because the body requires them in relatively large amounts. Vitamins and minerals are referred to as **micronutrients** because the body only needs them in small amounts.

Carbohydrates

Carbohydrates include **sugars**, **starches**, and **fiber**. Sugars are the simplest form of carbohydrate. They are made up of one or two sugar units. They taste sweet and are found in fruit, milk, and sweeteners like honey and table sugar. Starches are made of many sugar units that are linked together. They do not taste sweet, and are found in cereals, grains, and starchy vegetables like potatoes. Starches and sugars are good sources of energy in the diet and provide 4 calories per gram. Most fiber is also carbohydrate. Good sources of fiber include whole grains, legumes (peas and beans), fruits, and vegetables. Fiber provides little energy to the body because it cannot be digested or absorbed. It is, however, important for the health of the gastrointestinal tract.

Lipids

Lipids are commonly called fats. Fat is a concentrated source of energy in our diet and in our bodies, providing 9 calories per gram of fat. Most of the fat in our diet and in our bodies is in the form of **triglycerides**. Each triglyceride contains three **fatty acids**. Fatty acids are made up of chains of carbon atoms of varying lengths. Depending on how these carbons are linked together, fats are classified as either saturated or unsaturated. **Saturated fats** are usually solid at room temperature and are found mostly in animal products such as meat, milk, and butter. **Unsaturated fats** are found in

TABLE 1.1 CATEGORIES OF NUTRIENTS

Nutrient Category	Nutrients included
Macronutrients	
Carbohydrates	Sugars, starches and fiber
Protein	Proteins and amino acids
Lipids	Triglycerides, fatty acids, phosphoglycerides (phospholipids), and sterols (including cholesterol)
Water	Water
Micronutrients	
Vitamins	*Fat soluble vitamins:* vitamins A, D, E, and K *Water-soluble vitamins:* vitamins C, B_6, B_{12}, thiamin, riboflavin, folate, niacin, pantothenic acid, and biotin
Minerals	*Major minerals:* sodium, potassium, chloride, calcium, phosphorus, magnesium, and sulfur *Trace minerals:* iron, copper, zinc, manganese, selenium, iodine, fluoride, chromium, and molybdenum

vegetable oils and are usually liquid at room temperature. Small amounts of certain unsaturated fatty acids are essential in the diet. **Cholesterol** is another type of lipid found in animal foods. Diets high in saturated fat and cholesterol may increase the risk of heart disease. A type of unsaturated fat that is called **trans fat** should also be limited in the diet because it promotes heart disease.

Protein

Protein is needed for growth, maintenance and repair of body structures, and for the synthesis of regulatory molecules. It can also be broken down to provide energy (4 calories per gram of protein). Protein is made of folded chains of units called **amino acids**. The number and order of amino acids in the chain determine the type of protein. The right amounts and types of amino acids must be consumed in the diet in order to be able to build the proteins that the body needs. Animal foods such as meat, poultry, fish, eggs, and dairy products generally supply a combination of amino acids that meets human needs better than plant proteins do. However, vegetarian diets that contain only plant foods such as grains, nuts, seeds, vegetables, and legumes, can also meet protein needs.

Water

Water is an essential nutrient that makes up about 60% of the weight of an adult human body. It provides no energy, but it is needed in the body to transport nutrients, oxygen, waste products, and other important substances. It also is needed for many chemical reactions, for body structure and protection, and to regulate body temperature. Water is found in beverages as well as solid foods. Because water is not stored in the body, water intake must be balanced with water loss through urine, feces, sweat, and from evaporation to maintain proper hydration.

Vitamins

Vitamins are small, carbon-based molecules that are needed to regulate metabolic processes. They are found in almost all the foods we eat, but no one food is a good source of all of them. Some vitamins are soluble in water and others are soluble in fat, a property that affects how they are absorbed into and transported throughout the body. Vitamins do not provide energy, but the body needs many of them to regulate the chemical reactions that extract energy from sugars, fatty acids, and amino acids. Some vitamins are **antioxidants**, which protect the body from reactive oxygen compounds like **free radicals**. Others have roles in tissue growth and development, bone health, and blood clot formation.

Minerals

Minerals are single **elements** such as iron, calcium, zinc, and copper. Some minerals are needed in the diet in significant amounts, whereas the requirements for other minerals are extremely small. Like vitamins, minerals provide no energy, but they do perform a number of very diverse functions. Some of them are needed to regulate chemical reactions, some participate in reactions that protect cells from **oxidative damage**, and others have roles in bone formation and maintenance, oxygen transport, or immune function.

HOW MUCH OF EACH NUTRIENT DO YOU NEED?

To stay healthy, adequate amounts of energy and of each of the essential nutrients must be consumed in the diet. The amount of each nutrient that you need depends on your age, size, gender, genetic makeup, lifestyle, and health status. The **Dietary Reference Intakes (DRIs)** issued by the Food and Nutrition Board of the National Academy of Sciences' Institute of Medicine, are recommendations for the amounts of energy (calories), nutrients, and other substances that should be consumed on an average daily basis in order to promote health, prevent deficiencies, and reduce the incidence of chronic disease.

The Dietary Reference Intakes (DRIs)

The DRIs include recommendations for different groups of people based on their age, gender, and, when appropriate, whether they are pregnant or lactating. The recommendations for nutrient intake include four different types of values. The **Estimated Average Requirements (EARs)**, the first of these, are the amounts of nutrients that are estimated to meet the average needs of the population. EARs are not used to assess individual intake but rather are intended for planning and evaluating the adequacy of the nutrient intake of population groups. The next two, the **Recommended Dietary Allowances (RDAs)** and **Adequate Intakes (AIs)** are values that are calculated to meet the needs of nearly all healthy people in each gender and life-stage group. These values can be used to plan and assess the diets of individuals. The fourth set of DRI values is the **Tolerable Upper Intake Levels (ULs)**. These are the maximum levels of intake that are unlikely to pose a risk of adverse health effects. ULs can be used as a guide to limit intake and evaluate the possibility of excessive intake. When your diet provides the RDA or AI for each nutrient and does not exceed the UL for any of them, your risk of nutrient deficiency or toxicity is low.

The recommendations for energy intake are expressed as **Estimated Energy Requirements (EERs)**. These values predict the calories that are needed to maintain weight in healthy individuals. They are based on a person's age, gender, size, and activity level.

What Happens If You Get Too Little or Too Much?

Consuming either too much or too little of one or more nutrients or energy can cause **malnutrition**. Typically, we think of malnutrition as a lack of energy or nutrients. This occurs when there is not enough food and when the diet is not well planned, but it can also be caused by an increase in nutrient needs or an inability to absorb or use nutrients.

A deficiency of energy is called **starvation**. It causes a loss of body fat and muscle mass, resulting in an emaciated appearance. Malnutrition that is caused by a deficiency of an individual nutrient causes symptoms that reflect the functions of the nutrient in the body. For example, vitamin D is needed for strong bones. A deficiency of this vitamin causes children's leg bones to bow outward because they are too weak to support the body weight. Vitamin A is needed for healthy eyes and so a deficiency in this vitamin can result in blindness. For many nutrient deficiencies, supplying the lacking nutrient can quickly reverse the symptoms.

Overnutrition is an excess of energy or nutrients and also a form of malnutrition. An excess of energy causes **obesity**. Overnutrition also increases the risk of developing diseases such as **diabetes** and heart disease. Excesses of saturated fat, trans fat, cholesterol, and sodium can also increase the risk of heart dis-

TOO MUCH OF A GOOD THING CAN KILL YOU

We usually think of the vitamins and minerals in our supplements as a healthy addition to our diets, but taking too much of one or more vitamin or mineral can be dangerous. Large doses of vitamins and minerals from dietary supplements can cause problems including nerve damage, kidney stones, liver and heart damage, and in extreme cases, death. For example, high doses of vitamin B_6 can cause tingling, numbness, and muscle weakness; high doses of niacin can cause flushing; and too much vitamin C can cause diarrhea. Overdosing on iron from children's vitamin/mineral supplements is one of the leading causes of poisoning in children under the age of six. To be safe, take supplements according to the recommended doses and use the ULs from the DRIs to check for toxic doses.

ease. Excesses of vitamins and minerals rarely occur from eating food but they are seen with overuse of dietary supplements. For example, consuming too much vitamin B_6 can cause nerve damage and excess iron intake can cause liver failure.

TOOLS FOR CHOOSING A HEALTHY DIET

Knowing which nutrients your body needs to stay healthy is the first step in choosing a healthy diet, but knowing how many milligrams of niacin, micrograms of vitamin B_{12}, grams of fiber, or what percent of calories from carbohydrates should be included in a healthy diet doesn't help in deciding what to eat for breakfast or pack for lunch. A variety of tools have been developed to help make these kinds of choices. Three of them—standardized food labels, the Dietary Guidelines for Americans, and MyPyramid—are discussed in the sections that follow.

Understanding Food Labels

Food labels are a tool that is designed to help consumers make healthy food choices. They provide readily available information about the nutrient composition of individual foods and show how a serving of food fits into the recommendations for a healthy diet.

WHAT CAN YOU BELIEVE?

"Lose 10 pounds in a week!" Weight loss diets and products often make fabulous claims like this. But can you really believe everything you read? How can you tell what is fact and what is fantasy?

Generally, the rule is if it sounds too good to be true, it is. The following tips offer some suggestions for evaluating nutritional claims:

- **Think about it.** Does the information presented make sense? If not, disregard it.
- **Consider the source.** Where did the information come from? If it is based on personal opinions, be aware that one person's perception does not make something true.
- **Ponder the purpose.** Is the information helping to sell a product? Is it making a magazine cover or newspaper headline more appealing? If so, beware—the claims may be exaggerated to promote sales.
- **View the claim skeptically.** If a statement claims to be based on a scientific study, try to find out who did the study, what their credentials are, and what relationship they have to the product. Do the people who did the study benefit from the sale of the product?
- **Finally, evaluate the risks.** Find out what the risks of using the product are and be sure the expected benefit is worth the risk associated with using it.

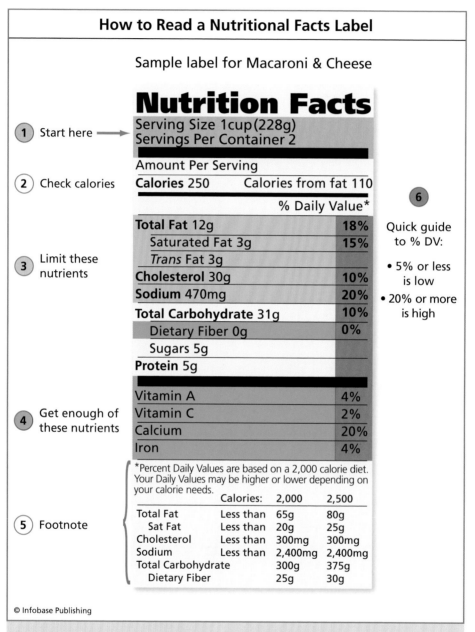

How to Read a Nutritional Facts Label

Sample label for Macaroni & Cheese

Nutrition Facts

(1) Start here → Serving Size 1cup(228g)
Servings Per Container 2

Amount Per Serving

(2) Check calories **Calories** 250   Calories from fat 110

% Daily Value*

Total Fat 12g	**18%**
Saturated Fat 3g	**15%**
Trans Fat 3g	
Cholesterol 30g	**10%**
Sodium 470mg	**20%**
Total Carbohydrate 31g	**10%**
Dietary Fiber 0g	**0%**
Sugars 5g	
Protein 5g	
Vitamin A	4%
Vitamin C	2%
Calcium	20%
Iron	4%

(3) Limit these nutrients

(4) Get enough of these nutrients

*Percent Daily Values are based on a 2,000 calorie diet. Your Daily Values may be higher or lower depending on your calorie needs.

	Calories:	2,000	2,500
Total Fat	Less than	65g	80g
Sat Fat	Less than	20g	25g
Cholesterol	Less than	300mg	300mg
Sodium	Less than	2,400mg	2,400mg
Total Carbohydrate		300g	375g
Dietary Fiber		25g	30g

(5) Footnote

(6) Quick guide to % DV:

• 5% or less is low

• 20% or more is high

© Infobase Publishing

FIGURE 1.2 Standard "Nutrition Facts" labels like this one appear on all packaged foods. They provide information about the number of calories and the amounts of fat, carbohydrates, and other nutrients that are in each serving of the packaged food. They can help you tell at a glance how much of each nutrient a particular food adds to your nutrient requirements.

Almost all packaged foods must carry a standard food label. The exceptions to this rule are raw fruits, vegetables, fish, meat, and poultry. For these foods, the nutrition information is often posted on placards in the grocery store or printed in brochures. Food labels must include both an ingredient list and a "Nutrition Facts" panel.

The "ingredient list" is a listing of all the substances that the food contains, including food additives, colors, and flavorings. The ingredients are listed in order of their prominence by weight. Therefore, a label that lists water first indicates that most of the weight of that food comes from water. The ingredient list is useful for those who need to avoid certain foods, such as animal products, or food to which they have an allergy.

The "Nutrition Facts" portion of a food label lists the serving size of the food followed by the total calories, calories from fat, total fat, saturated fat, trans fat, cholesterol, sodium, total carbohydrate, dietary fiber, sugars, and protein per serving of the food (Figure 1.2). The amounts of nutrients are given by weight and for most, also as a percent of the **Daily Value (DV)**. DVs are standards developed for food labels. They help consumers see how a food fits into their overall diet. For example, if a label notes that the food provides 10% of the Daily Value for fiber, then the food provides 10% of the daily recommendation for fiber intake in a 2,000-calorie diet. The amounts of vitamin A, vitamin C, iron, and calcium are also listed as a percent of the Daily Value.

In addition to the required nutrition information, food labels often highlight specific characteristics of a product that might be of interest to the consumer, such as whether it is "low in calories" or "high in fiber." The Food and Drug Administration (FDA) has developed definitions for these nutrient content descriptors. Food labels are also permitted to include specific health claims if they are relevant to the product. For example, the label on a package of oatmeal may claim that it helps to lower blood cholesterol. These claims are only permitted on labels if the scientific evidence for the claim has been reviewed by the FDA and found to be well supported.

The Dietary Guidelines

The Dietary Guidelines for Americans include recommendations that are designed to help people choose a diet and lifestyle that will promote health and reduce chronic disease risks. The Dietary Guidelines recommend choosing a variety of nutrient-dense foods. These include vegetables, fruits, whole grains, low-fat dairy products, lean meats, beans, nuts, and seeds. This type of diet is rich in fiber, micronutrients, and phytochemicals, and low in saturated and trans fats.

MyPyramid

MyPyramid is a tool designed to help consumers choose foods that meet the recommendations of the Dietary Guidelines. This

---

KEY RECOMMENDATIONS OF THE *DIETARY GUIDELINES FOR AMERICANS*

The key recommendations of the Dietary Guidelines are appropriate for all healthy Americans two years of age and older.

- Consume a variety of foods within and among the various food groups.
- Balance calorie intake with expenditure to manage body weight.
- Be physically active every day.
- Choose more fruits and vegetables, whole grains, and low-fat dairy products.
- Choose fats wisely.
- Choose fiber-rich carbohydrates and limit added sugars.
- Choose and prepare foods with little salt.
- If you drink alcoholic beverages, do so in moderation.
- Prepare, handle, and store food safely.

Source: USDA, 2005.

food guide divides foods into five food groups (grains, vegetables, fruits, milk, and meat and beans) and oils, based on the nutrients that they provide. The five food groups and oils are represented by the colored triangles that make up the pyramid. The shape of the pyramid helps emphasize the recommendations for the amounts of food from each of the five food groups

FOOD GROUPS BY THE NUMBERS

Using a food group system like MyPyramid to guide food intake in the United States is not new. The first food group system, or food guide, was published in 1916. It was called Food for Young Children and divided food into five groups: milk/meat, cereals, vegetables/fruits, fats/fatty foods, and sugars/sugary foods. During the Great Depression in the 1930s, a food guide consisting of 12 food groups was developed and released to help families save money on groceries. In 1943, shortages brought on by World War II led to the release a food guide called the "Basic Seven." But this food guide turned out to be rather complicated, so it was condensed to the Basic Four in 1956. The Basic Four included milk, meats, fruits and vegetables, and grain products and was used for the next 20 years. In the late 1970s, as concerns about the role of diet in chronic disease began to intensify, the USDA added a fifth category to the Basic Four: fats, sweets, and alcoholic beverages, all of which people were advised to consume in moderation. In 1992, the Food Guide Pyramid was introduced. It used a pyramid shape to emphasize the relative contribution that each food group should make to a healthy diet. It was replaced by MyPyramid in 2005.

Food guides are not unique to the United States. Those developed in other countries use a variety of shapes and numbers of groups to emphasize the proportions of different types of foods that should make up a healthy diet. Korea and China use a pagoda shape; Mexico, Australia, and most European countries use a pie or plate shape; and Canada uses a rainbow.

(Figure 1.4). Foods in the wider triangle columns of MyPyramid contain the most nutrients per calorie, which is referred to as **nutrient density.** Those in the narrow triangular columns have lower nutrient density. The figure climbing the pyramid is there to emphasize the importance of activity in maintaining nutritional health. Choosing the recommended amounts and varieties of foods from each group will provide a diet that meets nutrient recommendations and helps promote health, prevent disease, and support activity.

An individual MyPyramid plan can be found by going to www.mypyramid.gov and selecting MyPyramid Plan, and entering your age, gender, and activity level. The MyPyramid Web site also provides other interactive tools to help users identify their calorie needs, choose nutrient-dense foods, plan healthy diets, analyze what they are eating, and estimate the calories they expend in activity.

REVIEW

Food provides the human body with energy, in the form of calories, and nutrients, which are substances required in the diet for growth, reproduction, and maintenance. The right number of calories is needed to keep weight in the healthy range and the right combination of nutrients is needed to maintain health. There are six classes of nutrients. Carbohydrates include sugars, starches, and fibers; sugars and starches provide energy (4 calories per gram), while fibers provide little energy because they cannot be digested by human enzymes and therefore cannot be absorbed. Lipids are a concentrated source of calories in the diet

(opposite) **FIGURE 1.3** MyPyramid is designed to educate people about how much they should include form each food group in their diets. The amounts vary depending on individual calorie needs and can be obtained by going to www.mypyramid.gov and entering age, gender, and activity level.

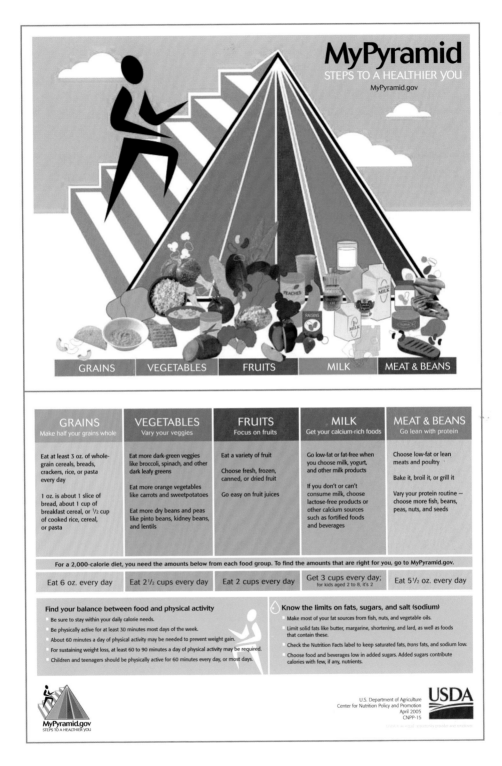

and in the body, providing 9 calories per gram—they are also needed to synthesize molecules that help regulate body processes. Proteins are made from amino acids. They can provide energy for the body, but they are more important for their structural and regulatory roles. Water is the most abundant nutrient in the body. Water intake must equal output to maintain balance. Vitamins and minerals are needed in the diet in small amounts. They both have regulatory roles, while some minerals also provide structure.

Consuming too much or too little energy or nutrients results in malnutrition. The Dietary Reference Intakes (DRIs) recommend the amounts of energy and nutrients that the body needs to promote health, prevent deficiencies, and reduce the incidence of chronic disease. Food labels, the Dietary Guidelines for Americans, and MyPyramid, provide information and recommendations that help people choose foods that make up a healthy diet.

CARBOHYDRATES

High-carbohydrate foods form the basis of diets around the world. For example, rice is the staple in the Asian diet, while pasta is often at the center of Italian cuisine, and corn or wheat tortillas play a major role in the Mexican diet. Whether the diet is eaten by a farmer in China or an aristocrat in England, the greatest proportion of the calories they consume generally comes from carbohydrates. This has been true for centuries. Nonetheless, diets high in carbohydrates have been blamed for everything from obesity to hyperactivity. Whether the carbohydrates we include in our diet promote our health or put it at risk depends on the type and source of the carbohydrate.

WHAT IS A CARBOHYDRATE?

The basic structural unit of a carbohydrate is a single sugar unit called a **monosaccharide**. The three most common monosaccharides in the diet are **glucose, fructose,** and **galactose**. Each of

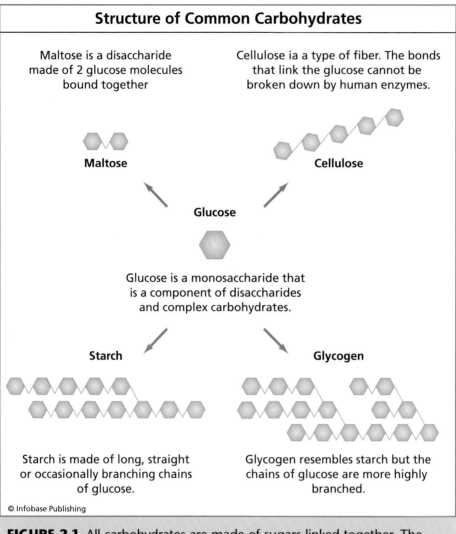

Structure of Common Carbohydrates

Maltose is a disaccharide made of 2 glucose molecules bound together

Cellulose ia a type of fiber. The bonds that link the glucose cannot be broken down by human enzymes.

Maltose

Cellulose

Glucose

Glucose is a monosaccharide that is a component of disaccharides and complex carbohydrates.

Starch

Glycogen

Starch is made of long, straight or occasionally branching chains of glucose.

Glycogen resembles starch but the chains of glucose are more highly branched.

© Infobase Publishing

FIGURE 2.1 All carbohydrates are made of sugars linked together. The structure of some common carbohydrates is illustrated here.

them contains 6 carbon, 12 hydrogen, and 6 oxygen atoms, but the arrangement of the atoms is different for each sugar. Glucose is the monosaccharide that travels in our bloodstream and is often called *blood sugar*. Fructose is a sugar found in fruit and is sometimes called *fruit sugar*. Galactose is a component of the sugar that is found in milk.

When two monosaccharides are linked together, they form a **disaccharide** (Figure 2.1). The most common disaccharides in the diet are **lactose**, **maltose**, and **sucrose**. Lactose is milk sugar. It is the only sugar found naturally in an animal product. It is made up of glucose linked to galactose. Maltose consists of two molecules of glucose and is formed when starch is broken down during digestion. Sucrose is what we know as common white sugar or table sugar; it is formed by linking glucose to fructose.

The monosaccharides and disaccharides are simple carbohydrates. When many sugar molecules are linked together, they form

EAT BEFORE YOU COMPETE

We store glycogen in our muscles and in our liver. The glycogen in muscles can be broken down to supply glucose to fuel muscle contraction during exercise. When liver glycogen is broken down, the glucose enters the blood and circulates to supply glucose to the muscles as well as the brain and other tissues throughout the body. To be at your best during exercise, your glycogen stores should be full when you begin. This could be a challenge if you exercise first thing in the morning after having not eaten for 8 to 12 hours. You do not eat while you are asleep and during this overnight fast, your muscles are resting, so the glycogen they have stored remains untouched. However, liver glycogen is needed to maintain blood glucose while you sleep. If you hit the pavement without having any breakfast you are literally running on empty. The glycogen in your muscles can provide glucose for muscle contraction, but to keep blood glucose in the normal range so your brain stays sharp, the liver will need to make glucose from other molecules. This may not be a problem when you take a quick morning jog, but if you are competing in the morning, you should get up early enough to eat a high-carbohydrate meal two to four hours before the competition to ensure your glycogen stores are full.

a **polysaccharide** (poly means "many"). Polysaccharides are complex carbohydrates. They include starch, fiber, and **glycogen**. Starch is an energy storage molecule for plants. It is made up of straight or branching chains of glucose molecules. Grains such as wheat and oats and starchy vegetables such as potatoes, beans, and corn, are sources of dietary starch. Fiber is also found in plant foods, such as grains, fruits, and vegetables. Fiber cannot be digested by human enzymes. (The importance of fiber in human health and nutrition will be discussed in Chapter 3). Glycogen, which is sometimes called animal starch, is a polysaccharide that is the storage form of glucose found in humans and other animals. It is made of glucose molecules linked together in highly branched chains. This branched structure allows it to be broken down quickly to release glucose into the blood when it is needed. We do not consume glycogen in our diets because it breaks down quickly after an animal dies.

CARBOHYDRATES IN THE HUMAN DIET

Carbohydrates make up more than 50% of the energy in a typical American diet. Some of these carbohydrates come from unrefined foods, meaning that the food has not been altered from its natural state or that it has only been minimally altered by processing. For example, corn on the cob is an unrefined source of carbohydrate, but corn flakes are a **refined** source. Today, much of the carbohydrates in the American diet is from refined grains and added refined sugar. Refined foods have undergone processing to remove certain parts of the original food. Recommendations for a healthy diet suggest that we eat more natural unrefined sources of carbohydrates and limit our consumption of refined grains and added sugars.

What are Whole Grains?

Most of the carbohydrates consumed in North America come from grains such as wheat, rice, and oats. A kernel of grain has three parts: the **bran**, the **germ**, and the **endosperm** (Figure 2.2).

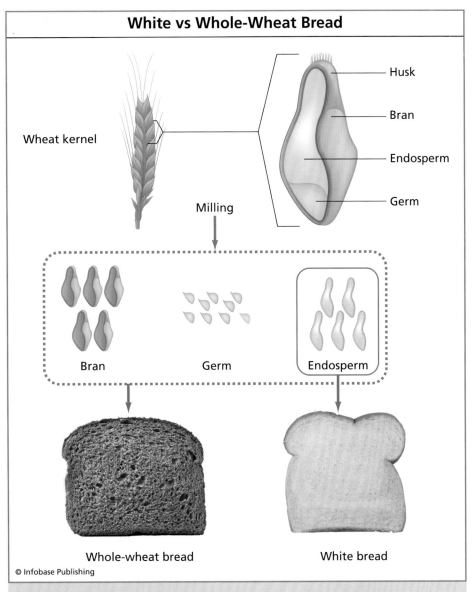

White vs Whole-Wheat Bread

Wheat kernel

Husk

Bran

Endosperm

Germ

Milling

Bran

Germ

Endosperm

Whole-wheat bread

White bread

© Infobase Publishing

FIGURE 2.2 A grain of wheat is made up of the high-fiber bran layers, the starchy endosperm, and the oil-rich germ. Milling separates these components. White flour is made from just the endosperm, but whole-wheat flour includes all parts of the wheat kernel.

The bran is the outer layers of the kernel. The layers are high in fiber and are also a good source of many vitamins and minerals. The germ is located at the base of the kernel and is the plant embryo where sprouting occurs. The germ is the source of plant oils and is rich in vitamin E. The largest portion of the kernel is called the endosperm. It is high in starch and contains most of the protein in the grain and some vitamins and minerals. Whole grain products, such as whole wheat bread, brown rice, and oatmeal, contain the entire kernel of the grain, including the bran, germ, and endosperm. Refined grain products, such as white bread and white rice, are made by removing the bran and the germ to produce a more uniform product. Removing the bran and germ, however, also removes most of the fiber and reduces the amounts of many of the vitamins and minerals. To identify products made primarily from whole grains look for the word "whole" before the name of the grain in the ingredient list. If this is the first ingredient in the ingredient list on the food label, the product is made mostly from whole grain.

Because nutrients are lost when the bran and germ are discarded, refined grains are enriched with certain vitamins and minerals. **Enrichment** is a type of fortification that adds some, but not all, of the nutrients lost in processing back to the grains. The B vitamins thiamin, riboflavin, niacin, and folic acid and the mineral iron are added to enriched grains in the United States, often to higher levels than originally present. However, vitamin B_6 and vitamin E, which are also lost in refining, are not added back. Refined grains therefore contain more of some nutrients and less of others than foods that are made from whole grains.

Added Sugars: Not So Sweet

Sugars are sweet, but eating too much added sugar is not. About 16% of the calories in the American diet are from refined sugar that is added to foods during processing or at the table. Refined sugar is sugar that has been separated from its plant sources so the fiber, vitamins, and minerals present in the original plant have been removed. Although refined sugars are chemically no different from natural ones, they add what we refer to as **empty calories** because when they are added to a food, they provide calories but no nutrients other than the carbohydrate. Foods that naturally contain sugars provide vitamins, minerals, fiber, and phytochemicals along with the calo-

THE CASE OF THE STRAWBERRY YOGURT

How much sugar is in a container of strawberry yogurt? It doesn't take a detective to find the answer. The number of grams of sugars in a serving is listed on the Nutrition Facts label. The strawberry yogurt label will indicate that a cup has 37 grams of sugars. But this number doesn't tell you whether the sugar came from the milk and strawberries used to make the yogurt, or if it was added to sweeten the final product.

The 37 grams listed on the label includes the fructose found naturally in strawberries, the lactose found naturally in milk, and any sugars added in processing. There is no way to know for sure from the Nutrition Facts label how much of the total is made up of added sugars. Sometimes a label will say "no added sugar" or "without added sugar," which tells you that no refined sugars were added in processing. The ingredient list provides some information about the sweeteners added to a food. While the amounts of ingredients are not given, the ingredients are listed in order of prominence by weight, so the closer an ingredient is to the front of the list, the more of it there is in the food. In strawberry yogurt, sugar is the second ingredient and high-fructose corn syrup, another common source of added sugar, is the fourth ingredient. The amount of added sugar is the sum of these two sources of sugar.

If you are looking for a product without added sugars, check the ingredients list and be sure you know the sugar terminology. All of the following are considered added sugar when they appear in the ingredient list: brown sugar, corn sweetener, corn syrup, dextrose, fructose, fruit juice, glucose, high-fructose corn syrup, honey, invert sugar, lactose, maltose, malt syrup, molasses, raw sugar, sucrose, and sugar syrup concentrates.

from the sugar. Natural unrefined sources of sugar include fruit, ich provides fructose, and dairy products, which are a source of lactose. Refined sugars include table sugar, high-fructose corn syrup, corn syrup, maltose, honey (which is refined by bees), and others. Because sucrose is the only sweetener that can be called "sugar" in the ingredient list on food labels in the United States, you need to know the names of other added sweeteners in order to see in the ingredient list if sugars have been added to a food.

HOW ARE CARBOHYDRATES DIGESTED?

To be absorbed into the body, all carbohydrates, whether simple or complex, must be broken down into monosaccharides. This breakdown, or digestion, occurs with the help of enzymes in the digestive tract. The digestion of starch begins in the mouth, where the enzyme salivary **amylase** breaks it into shorter polysaccharides. Starch digestion continues in the small intestine, where the action of pancreatic amylases breaks polysaccharides into maltose. Enzymes attached to the lining of the small intestine then complete the digestion of maltose and also break the disaccharides sucrose and lactose into monosaccharides. The resulting monosaccharides, glucose, galactose, and fructose, are then absorbed into the blood and transported to the liver.

Indigestible Carbohydrates

If carbohydrates in the small intestine are not completely broken down to monosaccharides, they cannot be absorbed and so they pass into the large intestine. There, the bacteria that normally live in this part of our gastrointestinal tract break down some of the carbohydrates. This produces acids, gas, and other by-products. Excessive amounts may cause abdominal discomfort and flatulence. Fiber is the most abundant indigestible carbohydrate in our food. Beans are a good source of fiber, but also contain other indigestible carbohydrates called **oligosaccharides**.

Oligosaccharides are the carbohydrates in beans that causes flatulence. These short polysaccharides cannot be completely digested by human enzymes and, thus, pass into the large intestine where they are broken down by bacteria. Some starch is also indigestible. Resistant starch is starch that escapes digestion in the small intestine because it is protected by the natural structure of the grain or because cooking alters its digestibility. Foods that are high in resistant starch include bananas, legumes, and cold cooked pasta, rice, and potatoes.

Lactose Intolerance

Lactose intolerance occurs when the level of lactase, the intestinal enzyme that breaks down lactose, is reduced. When someone with low lactase levels consumes milk, or other dairy products that contain lactose, the lactose is not digested and passes into the large intestine. Here, it draws in water and is metabolized by bacteria to produce acids and gas. The result is symptoms such as abdominal distension, flatulence, cramping, and diarrhea. All humans normally produce lactase at birth, but the enzyme's activity decreases with age; in many individuals, lactase activity declines so much that they are unable to completely digest lactose. It is estimated that about 25% of adults in the United States are lactose intolerant; the incidence is as high as 80% for African Americans, 80% to 100% for Native Americans, and 90% to 100% for Asian Americans.

Most individuals who are lactose intolerant can consume small amounts of lactose without experiencing symptoms. This is important because dairy products are the major source of calcium in the American diet, so when they are eliminated from the diet, it is difficult to meet calcium needs. People who can tolerate small amounts of lactose can meet their calcium needs by consuming small servings of milk and other dairy products throughout the day. Yogurt and cheese are dairy sources of calcium that are more easily tolerated than milk because some of the lactose in these products is digested or lost in processing. Those who cannot tolerate any lactose can choose nondairy sources of calcium such as tofu, legumes, leafy green vegetables, and fish consumed with bones. Lactose-free milk and lactase tablets, which digest the lactose before it passes into the large intestine, are also available.

WHAT DO CARBOHYDRATES DO?

Carbohydrates serve a number of functions in the body. The sugar galactose is needed in nervous tissue and to make lactose in breast milk; the monosaccharides deoxyribose and ribose are needed to make DNA and RNA, which contain genetic information and are needed for the synthesis of proteins; and short polysaccharides are important signaling molecules found on the surface of cells. However, the main role of carbohydrate, particularly glucose, is as an energy source: it provides about 4 calories per gram. Certain body cells, including brain cells and red blood cells, rely almost exclusively on glucose for energy.

Because of the key role that glucose plays in providing energy to body cells, hormones in the body carefully regulate the level of glucose in the blood, and therefore the amount of it that is available to the cells. Normal blood glucose levels are about 70 to 100 milligrams per 100 milliliters of blood. This level is regulated primarily by the hormones **insulin** and **glucagon**.

Lowering Blood Glucose

After a person eats a meal or snack containing carbohydrate, blood glucose levels rise. This rise triggers the **pancreas** to secrete insulin. Insulin promotes the uptake of glucose by body cells, where it can be used to provide energy or stored as glycogen for later use. This removes glucose from the blood, decreasing blood glucose levels to the normal range. How quickly blood glucose rises and how high it goes after carbohydrates are consumed depend on the amount and type of carbohydrate. Refined sugars and starches cause a quicker, greater rise in blood glucose than do unrefined sources of carbohydrate that contain fiber. This is because refined sugars and starches leave the stomach rapidly and are digested and absorbed quickly, causing a rapid rise in blood glucose. Fiber slows the emptying of the stomach and the absorption of glucose, so sources of unrefined carbohydrate, such as oatmeal, legumes, and whole grain bread cause a slower, lower rise in blood glucose. Including protein and fat with carbohydrates also slows glucose absorption. The disease diabetes occurs when there is not enough insulin, or the body does not respond to it, allowing blood glucose levels to remain high. High glucose concentrations can damage the eyes, the kidneys, and the circulatory and nervous systems.

Maintaining Blood Glucose Levels

When blood glucose levels drop too low, glucagon causes liver glycogen to break down, releasing glucose into the blood. Glucagon also stimulates liver and kidney cells to synthesize new glucose molecules by a process known as **gluconeogenesis.** Gluconeogenesis is important for meeting the body's need for glucose, but it can only use molecules containing 3 carbon atoms to synthesize glucose. These come primarily from amino acids found in body proteins. Glucose cannot be synthesized from fatty acids because they break down to form 2-carbon rather than 3-carbon molecules. Gluconeogenesis therefore uses up protein that could be used for other essential functions. When an adequate amount of carbohydrates are consumed in the diet, protein is not needed to synthesize glucose. Therefore, carbohydrates are said to spare protein.

CARBOHYDRATE METABOLISM: USING CARBOHYDRATES FOR ENERGY

Once glucose reaches the cells, it is broken down via a series of reactions called **cellular respiration** to produce carbon dioxide, water, and energy in the form of ATP. Cellular respiration involves four stages (Figure 2.3). The first stage occurs in the **cytoplasm** and is called **glycolysis.** In glycolysis, the 6-carbon sugar glucose is broken into two 3-carbon **pyruvate** molecules to produce two molecules of ATP. This stage is referred to as **anaerobic glycolysis** or **anaerobic metabolism** because it can proceed whether or not oxygen is available in the cell. This process produces ATP from glucose rapidly but inefficiently. What happens next to the pyruvate molecules depends on whether or not oxygen is available. When oxygen is unavailable, the pyruvate produced by anaerobic metabolism is converted to **lactic acid**. During intense exercise, lactic acid is produced in the muscles and can be transported in the blood and used as an energy source by other tissues. When oxygen is available, cellular respiration can proceed.

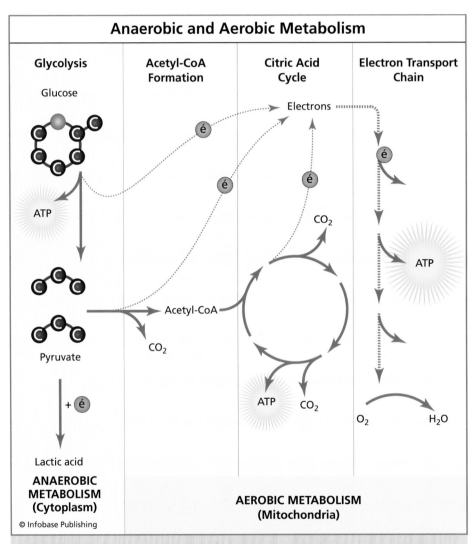

Anaerobic and Aerobic Metabolism

Glycolysis | Acetyl-CoA Formation | Citric Acid Cycle | Electron Transport Chain

Glucose

Electrons

é

é

é

é

ATP

CO_2

ATP

Acetyl-CoA

CO_2

Pyruvate

+ é

ATP

CO_2

O_2

H_2O

Lactic acid

ANAEROBIC METABOLISM (Cytoplasm)

AEROBIC METABOLISM (Mitochondria)

© Infobase Publishing

FIGURE 2.3 Glycolysis breaks glucose into 3-carbon molecules. In the presence of oxygen, these are converted to acetyl-CoA, which enters the citric acid cycle. High-energy electrons are released and transferred to the electron transport chain, where their energy is trapped to make ATP. When oxygen is absent, pyruvate combines with an electron to form lactic acid.

The remaining stages of cellular respiration take place in the **mitochondria**. In the second stage, pyruvate loses a carbon atom as carbon dioxide and combines with coenzyme A to form a molecule called acetyl-CoA. Acetyl-CoA then enters the third stage of cellular respiration, the **citric acid cycle**. Here, the molecule combines with a 4-carbon molecule called oxaloacetate to form citric acid, a 6-carbon molecule. In the citric acid cycle, two carbon atoms are removed as carbon dioxide until oxaloacetate is reformed. During these first three stages of cellular respiration, high-energy electrons are released. In the presence of oxygen, these electrons are passed to the final stage of cellular respiration, the **electron transport chain**. The electron transport chain accepts the electrons and passes them down a chain of molecules until they are finally combined with oxygen to form water. As the electrons are passed along, their energy is trapped and used to make ATP.

Because oxygen is required for the last three stages of cellular respiration to proceed, they are referred to as **aerobic metabolism**. Aerobic metabolism, which completely breaks down glucose to form carbon dioxide, water, and ATP, produces about 38 molecules of ATP per molecule of glucose. In contrast, when no oxygen is available and glucose is broken down by anaerobic metabolism, only two molecules of ATP are produced from each glucose molecule.

HEALTHY AND UNHEALTHY CARBOHYDRATES

A diet high in carbohydrates can be either good or bad for you, depending on the types of carbohydrates that are consumed, as well as the other components of the diet. In general, diets that are high in unrefined sources of carbohydrate, such as whole grains, fruits, and vegetables, are considered healthy because they are associated with a lower incidence of a variety of bowel disorders, heart disease, diabetes, and certain cancers. Diets high in added sugars and refined grains are generally considered unhealthy. This is because refined sources of carbohydrates are lower in nutrient density than unrefined sources. Unrefined carbohydrate sources,

DOES SUGAR MAKE PEOPLE HYPER?

Sugar consumption has been implicated as a cause of hyperactivity in children. When sugar is consumed, it causes a rapid rise in blood glucose, which is thought to fuel hyperactive behavior. However, research on sugar intake and behavior has failed to support the connection between sugar and hyperactivity. The hyperactive behavior observed after sugar consumption is likely to be due to other factors. For example, the excitement of a birthday party, rather than the sugar in the cake and ice cream, are more likely the cause of the hyperactive behavior. Other factors, including caffeine consumption, lack of either physical activity or sleep, the desire for more attention, and overstimulation, are likely to play a role.

such as brown rice, kidney beans, and bananas, are high in nutrient density because they provide many nutrients per calorie. Refined products that are high in added sugar, such as donuts, cakes, and cookies, are low in nutrient density because they contain few nutrients relative to the calories they provide. Diets high in refined carbohydrates and added sugar have been blamed for tooth decay, hyperactivity, obesity, and diabetes. Nutrition research supports the idea that carbohydrates play a role in some, but not all, of these conditions.

Does Sugar Cause Cavities?

The most common health problem associated with a diet that is high in sugar is **dental caries**, or cavities. Dental caries are formed when bacteria that live in the mouth metabolize sugar from the diet and produce acid. The acid can then dissolve the enamel and underlying structure of the teeth. Simple carbohydrates, particularly sucrose, cause cavities because they are easily broken down by these bacteria, but starch can also be metabolized by bacteria to produce acids that contribute to tooth decay. Preventing cavities requires proper dental hygiene, even when the diet is low in sugar.

Do Sweets and Starchy Foods Make You Fat?

Carbohydrates have been accused of contributing to weight gain. Based just on calories, this seems unlikely. Carbohydrates provide only 4 calories per gram compared to 9 calories per gram for fat. However, it has been suggested that because eating carbohydrates stimulates the release of insulin and insulin removes glucose from the blood and promotes energy storage, diets high in carbohydrates may increase both hunger and the storage of body fat. Low-carbohydrate diets cause less insulin release and also cause the production of molecules called ketones. **Ketones** are made when fat is broken down, and carbohydrate levels are low. Low blood insulin levels and elevated blood ketone levels suppress appetite. In addition, diets that are very low in carbohydrates can limit food choices so much that people eat less food because the diet is so monotonous. Weight is lost on low-carbohydrate diets because people consume fewer calories than they expend.

The type of carbohydrate is as important as the amount when it comes to insulin levels and weight loss. Refined carbohydrates are digested and absorbed very rapidly and cause a sharp rise in blood glucose and a corresponding rise in insulin levels. In contrast, unrefined carbohydrates, which are high in fiber, may actually promote weight loss because the fiber they provide makes people feel full after fewer calories are consumed. Fiber also slows the absorption of glucose and hence blunts the rise in insulin levels.

Do Refined Carbohydrates Cause Diabetes?

When refined starches and added sugars are consumed, blood glucose and, subsequently, insulin levels in the blood rise more sharply than when unrefined carbohydrates are eaten. Evidence is accumulating that long-term consumption of a diet that is high in refined starches and added sugars may increase the risk of developing type 2 diabetes. Type 2 diabetes is the form of the disease in which an insensitivity of body cells to insulin, a condition that is called insulin resistance, allows blood sugar

FIGURE 2.4 Your long-term health may be improved by replacing refined grains in your diet, such as the cookies and white bread in this photo, with less refined grain products, such as whole-grain muffins and whole-wheat bread.

levels to remain elevated. Studies have found that type 2 diabetes is less common in populations that consume diets high in unrefined grains than in populations that consume diets high in refined starches and added sugars (Figure 2.4). It is thought that over the long term the rise in insulin levels in response to a high intake of refined carbohydrates may increase the risk of developing diabetes.

HOW MUCH AND WHAT KIND OF CARBOHYDRATES DO YOU NEED?

In order to make sure that the body's cells receive glucose, a minimal amount of carbohydrates need to be consumed. To

HOW MANY CARBOHYDRATE CALORIES DO YOU EAT?

The DRIs recommend that adults consume between 45% and 65% of calories from carbohydrates, but how do you know the percentage in your diet? To find out, you need to know how many calories and how many grams of carbohydrates you eat each day. You can get this information by using a diet analysis computer program or food composition tables. Knowing that carbohydrates provide 4 calories per gram allows you to do the following calculation:

- Multiply the grams of carbohydrates by 4 calories per gram

Grams carbohydrates x 4 calories/gram carbohydrate = calories from carbohydrates

- Divide calories from carbohydrates by total calories in the diet and multiply by 100 to express as a percent

$$\frac{\text{Calories from carbohydrates}}{\text{Total calories}} \times 100 = \text{Percent calories from carbohydrates}$$

For example:
If your diet contains 2,000 calories and 300 g of carbohydrates

300 g of carbohydrates x 4 cal/g = 1,200 calories from carbohydrates

$$\frac{1,200 \text{ calories from carbohydrates}}{2,000 \text{ calories}} \times 100 = 60\% \text{ of calories from carbohydrates}$$

meet this need, the DRIs recommend the consumption of at least 150 grams of carbohydrates per day. However, in order to meet the body's energy needs without providing too much fat or protein, the diet should contain more than this—between 45% and 65% of calories from carbohydrates. This is equivalent to 225 to 325 grams of carbohydrates for someone who eats 2,000 calories a day.

The typical American diet contains the right percentage of calories from carbohydrate, but the types of carbohydrates that Americans consume do not meet public health guidelines. Recommendations suggest that we limit added sugar consumption, but it is estimated that about 16% of our calories come from added sugars in foods such as soft drinks, candy, and bakery products. It is recommended that half our grains be whole grains, but the average American consumes only one serving of whole grains per day. We can cut out added sugar by having fruit instead of baked goods for dessert, drinking water instead of soda, and switching to unsweetened breakfast cereal. Whole grain consumption can be increased by switching to whole-grain breads, brown rice, and whole-grain breakfast cereals.

SUGAR SUBSTITUTES : SATISFYING YOUR SWEET TOOTH

People who love sweets but don't like the calories these foods add to their diet might try artificial sweeteners. A 12-ounce, sugar-sweetened soft drink has about 150 calories. A soft drink made with artificial sweeteners has almost none. There are five artificial sweeteners commonly used in foods sold in the United States: saccharine, aspartame, Acelsufame K, sucralose, and stevia. They can sweeten food without adding many calories and they are generally safe for healthy people. If you replace some foods that are high in added sugars with artificially sweetened products, you can cut down on calories and decrease your sugar intake, but you will not necessarily make your diet healthier. Whether the soft drink is sweetened with sugar or artificial sweeteners, it provides no other nutrients to the diet.

REVIEW

Carbohydrates include sugars, starches, and fibers; sugars and starches provide energy, 4 calories per gram. **Simple carbohydrates** include single sugars called monosaccharides and double sugars called disaccharides. **Complex carbohydrates** are polysaccharides and include starches, fibers, and glycogen. Unrefined foods are those that have not been altered from their natural state. Healthy diets are full of unrefined sources of carbohydrates such as whole grains, fruits, and vegetables. Unrefined sources of sugar include fruit and milk. The **added refined sugar** found in candy, soda, and baked goods adds calories but few nutrients. To be absorbed from the digestive tract, carbohydrates must be digested into monosaccharides. In the body, glucose is metabolized to produce ATP, the energy source required by cells. To ensure a constant supply of glucose to body cells, blood glucose levels are regulated by the hormones insulin and glucagon. It is recommended that people consume a minimum of 150 grams of carbohydrates per day, but a more realistic goal is 45 to 65% of calories from carbohydrates. This should come primarily from whole grains, fruits, vegetables, and milk with limited amounts of added sugars. A diet that meets these recommendations may reduce the risk of diabetes, obesity, and dental caries.

3

DIETARY FIBER

"**E**at your roughage," was a common piece of advice that your grandmother's generation passed on to their children. Today, the advice remains the same, but what they called roughage is what we call fiber. Fiber is plant matter that cannot be digested by human enzymes. We consume it whenever we eat whole grains, legumes, fruits, and vegetables. Because we cannot digest fiber, it moves through the entire digestive system and much of it winds up being excreted in the feces. Yet, even though our bodies do not absorb fiber, it is important to our health.

TYPES OF FIBER IN THE DIET

Fiber includes a number of chemical substances that have different physical properties and different physiological effects in the body. Most fibers are carbohydrates. Lignin is an exception. It is chemically not a carbohydrate, but it is classified as fiber because of how it behaves in the digestive tract. Fibers have been traditionally categorized based on their solubility in water.

Insoluble fibers do not dissolve in water. These fibers are derived primarily from the structural parts of plants. Chemically, they include lignin and cellulose and some hemicelluloses. Dietary sources of insoluble fiber include wheat bran and rye bran, and vegetables such as celery and broccoli.

Soluble fibers form viscous solutions when placed in water. The soluble fiber in oats gives cooked oatmeal its thick gelatinous consistency. Soluble fibers are found in and around plant cells and include pectins, gums, and some hemicelluloses. Food sources of soluble fibers include oats, apples, beans, and seaweed. Soluble fibers are often added to foods in processing. Pectin is used to thicken jams and jellies. Gums, such as gum arabic, gum karaya, guar gum, and locust bean gum are extracted from shrubs, trees, and seed pods and are added to foods like mayonnaise, yogurt,

FIGURE 3.1 Soluble and insoluble fibers help improve digestion and prevent diseases. These two types of fiber can be found in fruits, vegetables, and grain products such as whole-wheat bread.

TABLE 3.1 DIETARY SOURCES OF SOLUBLE AND INSOLUBLE FIBER

Food/Serving	Total Fiber (g)	Insoluble Fiber (g)	Soluble Fiber (g)	Energy (Cal)
Wheat bran flakes, 1 cup	6.15	5.52	0.63	126
Broccoli, 1 cup	2.8	1.4	1.4	28
Celery, 1 stalk	0.29	0.19	0.10	3
Oatmeal, 1 cup	4.00	2.15	1.85	145
Apple, 1 medium	3.73	2.76	0.97	81
Carrot, 1 medium	1.84	0.92	0.92	26
Plum, 1 medium	0.99	0.46	0.53	36
Kidney beans, 1/2 cup	5.72	2.86	2.86	113
Green peas, 1/2 cup	4.40	3.12	1.28	62
Metamucil, 1 tbsp	5.10	1.05	4.05	21

and cake as stabilizers and thickeners. Agar, carrageenan, and alginates come from seaweed, and are used as thickeners and stabilizers in foods like salad dressing and ice cream. Pectins and gums are also used in reduced-fat products because they mimic the slippery texture of fat. Most foods of plant origin contain mixtures of soluble and insoluble fibers (Figure 3.1 and Table 3.1).

WHAT HAPPENS TO FIBER IN THE DIGESTIVE TRACT?

Soluble and insoluble fiber behave somewhat differently in the gastrointestinal tract. Soluble fiber absorbs water and form viscous solutions that slow the rate at which nutrients are absorbed from the small intestine. Because neither soluble nor insoluble fiber can be digested in the small intestine, they cannot be absorbed and so they travel into the large intestine. Bacteria in the **colon** digest soluble fiber to produce gas and fatty acids, small quantities of which are absorbed and affect other functions in the body. Some soluble fiber—and most insoluble fiber—is excreted in the feces.

Insoluble fibers do not absorb water and are not broken down by bacteria, but they do increase the amount of material in the intestine. When insoluble and soluble fiber are consumed together, the increased bulk of the insoluble fiber and the extra water held by the soluble fiber increase the volume of material in the intestine. The larger, softer mass of material strengthens the muscles of the colon by stimulating **peristalsis**, which is the rhythmic muscle contractions that propel food through the digestive tract. A high-fiber diet allows the stool to pass easily and reduces **transit time**, which is the time it takes for food and fecal matter to move through the gastrointestinal tract.

FIBER GETS THINGS MOVING

A high-fiber diet increases the volume of fecal matter and the rate at which it moves through the gastrointestinal tract. A study done in the 1970s that compared the transit times and stool weights of African villagers who ate a high-fiber diet with British people who ate a low-fiber diet dramatically illustrated fiber's effect. It took an average of only about 35 hours for material to pass through the digestive tracts of the African villagers, but it took almost 70 hours for material to move through the digestive tracts of the British citizens. Dramatic differences were also seen in stool weight. The Africans who ate the high-fiber diets had an average daily stool weight of about 480 grams in contrast to only about 110 grams for the British who consumed the low-fiber diet.

HOW DOES FIBER AFFECT YOUR HEALTH?

A diet high in fiber has beneficial effects on the health of the gastrointestinal tract and can relieve or prevent some chronic health problems. When a high-fiber diet is consumed, the feces are larger and softer and the amount of pressure needed for def-

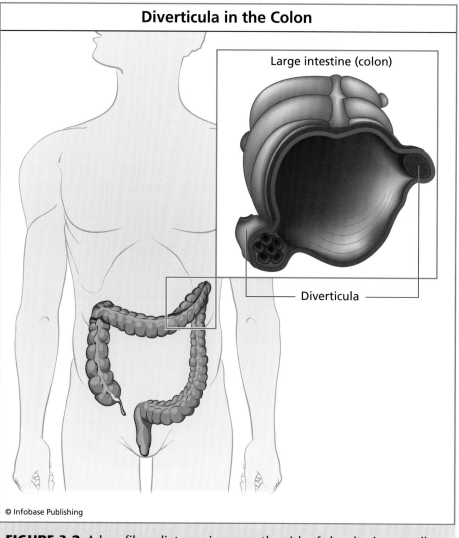

Diverticula in the Colon

Large intestine (colon)

Diverticula

© Infobase Publishing

FIGURE 3.2 A low-fiber diet can increase the risk of developing small pouches, or diverticula, in the colon. If stool gathers in these small pockets, it could lead to pain and infection.

ecation is reduced. This helps reduce the incidence of constipation, which refers to infrequent stools that are dry and difficult to pass. It also prevents hemorrhoids, which are swellings of the **veins** in the rectal or anal area. The reduced pressure in the large intestine also reduces the risk of **diverticulosis** (Figure 3.2). This is a condition in which pressure causes outpouchings called diverticula to form in the wall of the large intestine. If fecal matter accumulates in these outpouchings, it can cause irritation, pain, inflammation, and infection, a condition known as diverticulitis. A high-fiber diet can also be beneficial for weight management because fiber makes a person feel full with less food.

KELLOGG'S CORN FLAKES: A HEALTH FOOD?

The idea that fiber is good for health is not new. Dr. John Harvey Kellogg believed that problems with the bowel and stomach were the cause of the majority of ailments. He thought that people developed a condition called "autointoxication" by eating meat, drinking alcohol and coffee, smoking, and overindulging in sex, spicy foods, and a variety of other activities. Kellogg treated the rich and famous for a host of medical complaints at his Battle Creek Sanitarium (known as "the San") in Michigan. He advocated vigorous exercise, sexual abstinence, and a high-fiber vegetarian diet, along with daily enemas to clean out the bowels. On March 7, 1897, Dr. Kellogg dished up the first serving of corn flakes at the San. These were an unsweetened addition to the diets of Dr. Kellogg's patients and were not the same corn flakes that you can buy today. The corn flakes we recognize today made their appearance in 1906. They were the brainchild of Dr. Kellogg's brother, Will Keith Kellogg, who added sugar to the recipe and began marketing them as a breakfast food. John Harvey Kellogg was not supportive of this development and actually sued his brother in a failed attempt to keep the Kellogg name off mass-produced breakfast cereals.

Fiber and Heart Disease

A diet that is high in fiber can help reduce the risk of heart disease. Soluble fibers such as those in legumes, rice and oat bran, gums, pectin, and psyllium (a grain used in over-the-counter, bulk-forming laxatives such as Metamucil) help reduce the risk of heart disease by lowering blood cholesterol levels. Cholesterol in the blood comes from both cholesterol made in the liver and cholesterol consumed in animal products in the diet. One thing the body uses cholesterol for is to make **bile acids,** which are secreted into the GI tract to aid in the absorption of dietary fat. Normally, these bile acids are then reabsorbed and reused, thereby recycling the cholesterol. However, soluble fiber binds to bile acids and cholesterol in the GI tract, causing them both to be excreted in the feces rather than being absorbed (Figure 3.3). The liver must then use cholesterol from the blood to synthesize new bile acids, thereby reducing blood cholesterol levels.

Insoluble fiber, such as that found in wheat bran, does not lower blood cholesterol, but a high-fiber diet in general helps protect against heart disease. One study found that every additional 10 grams of fiber in the diet reduced the incidence of heart disease by 17%. In addition to lowering blood cholesterol, diets high in fiber help to lower blood pressure, normalize blood glucose levels, prevent obesity, and affect a number of other parameters that help reduce the risk of heart disease.

Fiber and Diabetes

A high-fiber diet is beneficial for the prevention and management of diabetes. The added bulk and thick solutions formed by fiber in the intestine slows the absorption of glucose. Therefore, blood glucose levels will rise more slowly with a carbohydrate-containing meal that is high in fiber. This decreases the amount of insulin needed to keep glucose in the normal range. This is beneficial for managing blood glucose in individuals with diabetes and, over the long term, is believed to reduce the risk of developing the disease. In fact, studies have found that diets high in fiber are associated with a lower incidence of diabetes.

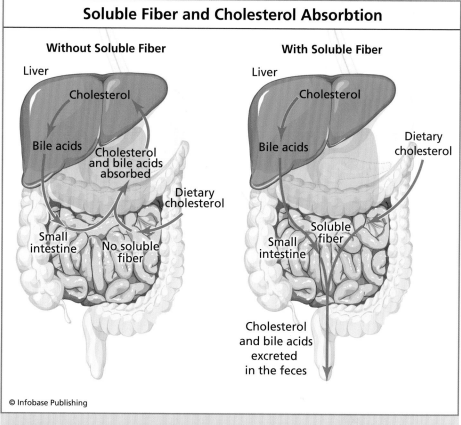

Soluble Fiber and Cholesterol Absorbtion

Without Soluble Fiber

Liver

Cholesterol

Bile acids
Cholesterol
and bile acids
absorbed

Dietary
cholesterol

Small
intestine

No soluble
fiber

With Soluble Fiber

Liver

Cholesterol

Bile acids

Dietary
cholesterol

Soluble
fiber

Small
intestine

Cholesterol
and bile acids
excreted
in the feces

© Infobase Publishing

FIGURE 3.3 A diet high in soluble fiber reduces the absorption of bile acids and cholesterol from the small intestine. This lowers cholesterol in the bloodstream and reduces the risk of heart disease.

Fiber and Colon Cancer

Adequate dietary fiber may protect against colon cancer. Epidemiological studies have shown that colon cancer incidence is lower in populations that consume high-fiber diets. This may occur because fiber dilutes the intestinal contents and speeds the rate at which material moves through the intestines. Together, these effects decrease the amount of time that the cells lining the colon are exposed to potentially cancer-causing substances present in the intestinal contents. The presence of fiber in the large intestine may also change the type of bacteria that grow there and the substances that are produced by the bacteria as they break down material in the colon. These substances may directly affect cells in the colon. Some of the effect of a high-fiber diet in preventing colon cancer may also be due to substances other than

BACTERIA IN THE INTESTINE

Amazingly, the large intestine is home to several hundred species of bacteria. Our bodies provide them with a nice warm home with lots of food and they do you some favors in return—that is, if they are the right kind of bacteria. The right intestinal bacteria improve the digestion and absorption of essential nutrients, synthesize some vitamins, and metabolize harmful substances, such as ammonia, thus reducing levels in the blood. Bacteria are important for intestinal immune function, proper growth of cells in the large intestine, and optimal movement through the GI tract. A healthy population of intestinal bacteria may also help prevent constipation, gas, and excess stomach acid. However, if the wrong bacteria take over, the result could be diarrhea, infections, and perhaps an increased risk of cancer.

How can people make sure the right bacteria live in their gut? One way is to eat them. This is referred to as **probiotic** therapy. Live bacteria are found in foods such as yogurt and acidophilus milk, and they can be purchased as bottled suspensions or tablets. However, one problem with probiotic therapy is that the bacteria are washed out of the colon once the user stops eating them. A second approach that can ensure that healthy bacteria are growing in the gut is the consumption of foods or other substances that encourage the growth of these particular types of bacteria. Called **prebiotics**, these substances pass undigested into the large intestine and serve as food for the healthy bacteria that live there. Prebiotics are sold as dietary supplements, but don't run to the store just yet. For most of us, simply eating a healthy diet will support a healthy population of intestinal bacteria.

fiber that are present in high-fiber foods. Not all studies support a role for fiber in reducing the incidence of colon cancer, but for most people there is no disadvantage in consuming a high-fiber diet as long as their fluid intake is adequate.

PROBLEMS WITH HIGH-FIBER DIETS

A high-fiber diet can cause problems if fluid intake is not sufficient, or if fiber intake is increased too rapidly. High-fiber diets also have the potential to affect vitamin and mineral levels and calorie intake.

Consuming fiber without consuming enough fluid can cause constipation. Fiber increases the need for water because it holds fluid in the gastrointestinal tract. The more fiber there is in the diet, the more water is needed to keep the stool soft. When too little fluid is consumed, the stool becomes hard and difficult to eliminate. Intestinal blockage can occur in severe cases when fiber intake is excessive and fluid intake is low. To avoid these problems, the fluid content of the diet should be increased when fiber consumption increases. Even when there is plenty of fluid, a sudden increase in fiber intake can cause abdominal discomfort, gas, and diarrhea due to the bacterial breakdown of fiber. To avoid these problems, fiber intake should be increased gradually.

In some people, a diet high in fiber can increase the risk of vitamin and mineral deficiencies. This occurs for two reasons. First, the increase in the volume of intestinal contents that occurs with a high-fiber diet may prevent enzymes from coming in contact with food. If a food cannot be broken down, the vitamins and minerals from that food cannot be absorbed. Second, fiber may bind some minerals, preventing their absorption. For instance, wheat bran fiber binds zinc, calcium, magnesium, and iron, reducing their absorption. A high-fiber diet can contribute to deficiencies when the overall diet is low in micronutrients. High-fiber diets are of concern in children because they have small stomachs and high nutrient needs. Children consuming a diet that is very high in fiber may feel full before they have met all their energy and nutrient needs.

HOW MUCH FIBER DO YOU NEED?

Most Americans do not eat enough fiber. The typical American diet contains only about 15 grams per day while the DRIs recommend a daily intake of 25 grams for young adult women and 38 grams for young adult men. This recommendation refers to total fiber, which includes dietary fiber and functional fiber. Dietary fiber is found intact in plant foods. Functional fiber is fiber that has been isolated from foods and shown to have beneficial physiological effects in humans. For example, the oat bran added to breads and breakfast cereals is functional fiber. Increasing your fiber intake means increasing your intake of plant foods that have only been minimally refined, such as fresh fruits and vegetables and whole grain products. People can also increase fiber intake by consuming foods with added functional fiber such as cereal that contains added oat bran or flax seed.

REVIEW

Fiber cannot be digested by human enzymes in the gastrointestinal tract, so it is not absorbed into the body. Nonetheless, a diet high in fiber is important to human health. Fiber is classified as either soluble or insoluble. Soluble fiber absorbs water and forms viscous solutions. It slows nutrient absorption and helps reduce blood cholesterol levels. In the large intestine, soluble fiber can be broken down by intestinal bacteria producing gas and acids, some of which can be absorbed into the body. Insoluble fiber is not broken down by intestinal bacteria and adds bulk to intestinal contents. The added bulk stimulates intestinal motility and strengthens muscles in the colon. A high-fiber diet, when consumed with adequate fluid, reduces the risk of constipation and diverticulosis because stools are softer and less pressure is needed for defecation. A high-fiber diet may also reduce the risk of heart disease, diabetes, and colon cancer. Americans currently do not consume the recommended amounts of fiber.

LIPIDS

It is cream that gives ice cream its smooth texture and rich taste, and olive oil that gives Italian food its distinctive aroma and flavor. Cream, oils, and other fats contribute to the texture, flavor, and aroma of our food. While we crave fats for their taste and texture, we are told to avoid them because too much fat—or at least too much of some types of fat—may increase our risk for heart disease, cancer, and obesity.

TYPES OF FATS

The term *fat* usually refers to lipids, but what we are most often referring to with this term are types of lipids called triglycerides. Most of the lipids in our food and in our bodies are triglycerides. The structure of a triglyceride includes lipids called fatty acids. **Phospholipids** and **sterols** are two other types of lipids that play an important role in human nutrition.

Triglycerides and Fatty Acids

A triglyceride is made up of three fatty acids attached to a 3-carbon molecule called glycerol (Figure 4.1). (When one fatty acid is attached, the molecule is called a monoglyceride; when two fatty acids are attached, it is a diglyceride.) Triglycerides may contain any combination of fatty acids. Their fatty acid composition determines their taste, texture, physical character-istics, and health effects.

Fatty acids consist of chains of carbon atoms linked together. Some fatty acids contain only a few carbons in this chain; others may have 20 carbons or more. Each carbon atom in the fatty acid chain forms four **chemical bonds** that can link it to as many as four other atoms. At one end of the chain, the omega end, the carbon atom is attached to its neighboring carbon and 3 hydro-gen atoms to form a methyl group (CH_3); at the other end of the chain, the last carbon is part of an acid group (COOH). Each of the carbons in between is attached to 2 other carbons and up to 2 hydrogen atoms. When each carbon in the fatty acid chain is bound to 2 hydrogen atoms, it is a called a saturated fatty acid because the carbon chain is saturated with hydrogen atoms. If the chain contains carbons that are not bound to 2 hydrogen atoms, a double bond is formed between 2 carbons. Fatty acids containing one or more double bonds are called unsaturated fatty acids.

Saturated Fats

Triglycerides containing a high proportion of saturated fatty acids are referred to as saturated fats. Saturated fats are found primarily in animal foods such as meat, milk, and cheese. They are also found in palm oil, palm kernel oil, and coconut oil. These saturated vege-table oils are often called **tropical oils** because they are from plants that commonly grow in tropical climates. They are used by the food industry in cereals, crackers, salad dressings, and cookies because saturated oils are more resistant to spoilage and therefore have a

Triglycerides and Fatty Acids

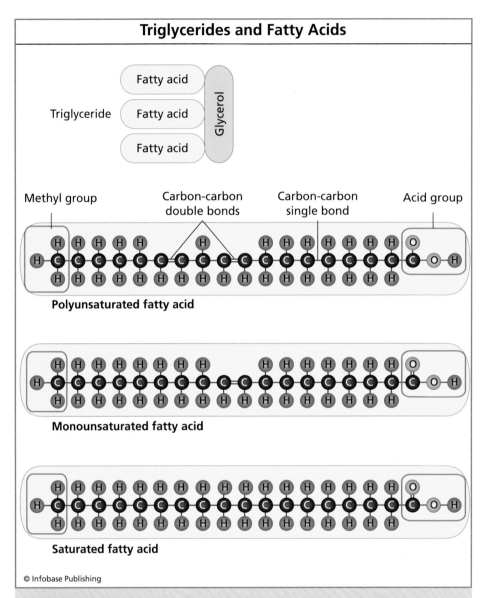

FIGURE 4.1 A triglyceride is made up of three fatty acids attached to a molecule of glycerol. The fatty acids in the triglyceride may be saturated (no carbon-carbon double bonds), monounsaturated (one carbon-carbon double bond), or polyunsaturated (more than one carbon-carbon double bonds).

longer shelf life than unsaturated oils. Diets high in saturated fats are associated with an increased risk of heart disease.

Unsaturated Fats

Unsaturated fats are triglycerides that contain a high proportion of unsaturated fatty acids. Unsaturated fatty acids contain one or more unsaturated (double) bonds. Those that contain one carbon-carbon double bond are called **monounsaturated fatty acids (MUFA)**. Oils that are high in monounsaturated fatty acids include olive, peanut, and canola oils. Fatty acids with more than one double bond in their carbon chains are called **polyunsaturated fatty acids (PUFA)**. Good sources of polyunsaturated fatty acids include corn, soybean, and safflower oils. Diets high in mono- and polyunsaturated fats are associated with a reduced risk of heart disease.

A type of unsaturated fatty acid that is not good for your heart is trans fat. Trans fatty acids are found in small amounts in nature and in larger amounts in **hydrogenated fats**. Food manufacturers use **hydrogenation** to increase the shelf life of oils. Hydrogenation is a process that adds hydrogen atoms to unsaturated fatty acids, converting some carbon-carbon double bonds to saturated bonds. This makes the fat more solid at room temperature and less likely to spoil. However, it also changes some of the carbon-carbon double bonds that remain. Most unsaturated fatty acids have carbon-carbon double bonds with both hydrogen atoms on the same side of the bond. This is known as the cis configuration. Hydrogenation results in trans fatty acids, which have carbon-carbon double bonds with the hydrogen atoms on opposite sides of the double bond (Figure 4.2).

Unsaturated fatty acids are categorized based on the location of the first double bond in the carbon chain. If the first double bond occurs after the sixth carbon (from the omega, or CH_3, end) the fat is said to be an **omega-6 fatty acid**. The major omega-6 fatty acid in the American diet is **linoleic acid**, which is plentiful in vegetable oils. Omega-6 fatty acids are important for growth,

skin integrity, fertility, and maintaining red blood cell structure. Unsaturated fatty acids with the first double bond after the
third carbon, counting from the omega (CH_3) end of the chain,

Cis and Trans Double Bonds

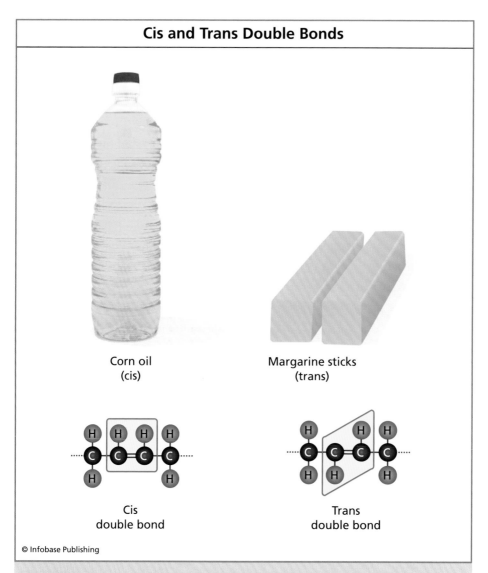

Corn oil
(cis)

Margarine sticks
(trans)

Cis
double bond

Trans
double bond

© Infobase Publishing

FIGURE 4.2 In a cis double bond, the hydrogen atoms are on the same
side of the double bond. In a trans double bond, the hydrogen atoms are
on opposite sides. During the hydrogenation of vegetable oils to make
margarine and shortening, some of the cis bonds are converted to trans.

are called **omega-3 fatty acids. Alpha-linolenic acid,** found in vegetable oils, and **eicosapentaenoic acid (EPA)** and **docosahexaenoic acid (DHA),** found in fish oils, are omega-3 fatty acids. Omega-3 fatty acids play an important role in the structure and function of **cell membrane**s, particularly those in the retina of the eye and the central nervous system. Diets high in omega-3 fatty acids help reduce the risk of heart disease. Supplements containing fish oils or purified omega-3 fatty acids are marketed to lower heart disease risk although they are not as effective as consuming a diet high in fish that contains omega-3 fatty acids.

Essential Fatty Acids

Because the human body is unable to synthesize double bonds in the omega-6 and omega-3 positions, linoleic acid (omega-6) and alpha-linolenic acid (omega-3) are **essential fatty acids** and must be included in the diet. They can be used to make other omega-6 and omega-3 fatty acids. For example, if the diet is low in linoleic acid, the body cannot make the omega-6 fatty acid, known as arachi-

FIXING INFANT FORMULAS

Docosahexaenoic acid (DHA) and arachidonic acid are important components of the central nervous system and the retina of the eye. DHA is an omega-3 fatty acid that can be made in the body from alpha-linolenic acid, and arachidonic acid is an omega-6 fatty acid that can be made from linoleic acid. An infant's body, particularly a premature infant's, may make these fatty acids at too slow a rate to support optimal brain and retinal development. This is not a problem in breast-fed infants because DHA and arachidonic acid are plentiful in breast milk. Does this mean that breast-fed babies are smarter and can see better? Not necessarily, but to optimize infant nutrition, some infant formulas are now fortified with these fatty acids. These formulas are recommended for premature infants.

donic acid, and so it becomes a dietary essential. EPA and DHA are omega-3 fatty acids that are synthesized from alpha-linolenic acid.

People who do not consume essential fatty acids in adequate amounts are likely to suffer from symptoms of **essential fatty acid deficiency**. These symptoms include scaly, dry skin; liver abnormalities; wounds that heal poorly; and impaired vision and hearing. Infants with this deficiency fail to grow properly. Luckily, essential fatty acid deficiency is rare because the human body's requirement for essential fatty acids is well below the amounts that people typically consume.

Phospholipids

Phospholipids are important in foods and in the body because they allow water and oil to mix. They consist of a backbone of glycerol with two fatty acids and a phosphate group attached (Figure 4.3). (A phosphate group is a chemical group containing the mineral phosphorous.) The negative chemical charge on the phosphate end of the phospholipid molecule allows this end to dissolve in water. In contrast, the fatty acid end of the molecule is soluble in fat. In foods, phospholipids act as **emulsifiers**, which are substances that break oils into small droplets so they can mix with watery ingredients. For example, the phospholipid **lecithin** is used in salad dressings to keep the oil and water portions from separating.

In the body, phospholipids form the structure of cell membranes. Cell membranes consist of two layers of phospholipid molecules called a **lipid bilayer**. The molecules are oriented so that the water-soluble phosphate end of the phospholipid molecules faces the watery environments inside and outside of the cell and the fat-soluble fatty acids face each other. This allows an aqueous environment both inside and outside the cell with a lipid environment sandwiched between them.

Cholesterol and Other Sterols

Cholesterol is probably the best-known sterol. Sterols are lipids that have chemical rings as the basis of their structure. In the body, cholesterol is part of both cell membranes and the insulating sheath

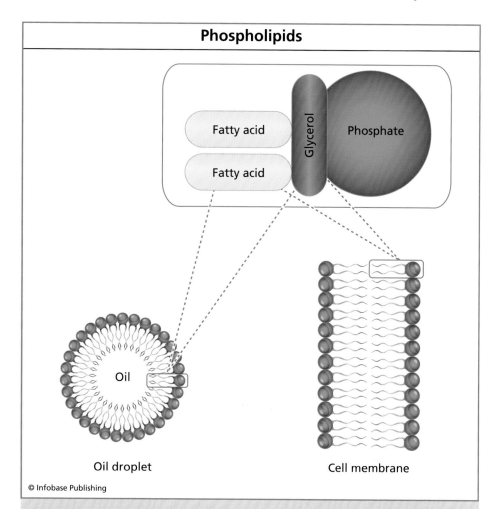

Phospholipids

© Infobase Publishing

Oil droplet

Cell membrane

Oil

Fatty acid

Fatty acid

Glycerol

Phosphate

FIGURE 4.3 Phospholipids have a water-soluble head, containing a phosphate group, and a fat-soluble tail of fatty acids. In food, such as salad dressing, they act as emulsifiers by surrounding lipid droplets so they stay suspended in water. In the body, they form the basic structure of cell membranes.

that covers the nerves and is needed for proper nerve function. Cholesterol is also needed to synthesize vitamin D, bile acids, and a number of hormones, including the sex hormones. Although it is essential in the body, cholesterol is not a dietary essential because it is made in the liver. Dietary cholesterol is found only in animal foods such as meats, eggs, and dairy products. Plant foods do not contain cholesterol, but they do contain other types of sterols. A diet high in cholesterol can increase the risk of heart disease.

WHAT DO LIPIDS DO?

Lipids are an important structural component of cell membranes, particularly in the brain and nervous system. Lipids also have important regulatory roles. The lipid cholesterol is used to synthesize certain hormones, such as the sex hormones, and fatty acids are used to make hormone-like molecules called **eicosanoids**. Eicosanoids help regulate blood clotting, blood pressure, immune function, and other body processes. The effect that an eicosanoid has on these parameters depends on whether it is made from an omega-3 or an omega-6 fatty acid. For example, eicosanoids made from omega-3 fatty acids will lower **blood pressure** and those made for omega-6 fatty acids will raise blood pressure. Therefore, it is important to consume a diet that includes a healthy balance of omega-3 and omega-6 fatty acids.

Fat is also an important energy source. Triglycerides consumed in the diet can be used as an immediate source of energy or be stored in the adipose tissue for future use. Because triglycerides are a concentrated energy source (9 calories per gram), they can store a large amount of energy in the body without a great increase in body size or weight. Adipose tissue also insulates the body from changes in temperature, and provides a cushion to protect against shock.

DIGESTING, ABSORBING, AND TRANSPORTING LIPIDS

Because most fats do not dissolve in water, they require special treatment during digestion, absorption, and transport throughout the body. Most lipid digestion takes place in the small intestine through the action of enzymes that are called **lipases**. Digestion and absorption of lipids are aided by **bile**. Bile is produced in the liver and stored in the **gallbladder**. It contains bile acids and helps break fat into small globules that can be accessed more easily by digestive enzymes. The enzymes break triglycerides into fatty acids, glycerol, and monoglycerides. The fatty acids and monoglycerides mix with bile and other lipids to form tiny droplets called **micelles**, which facilitate fat absorption.

After their absorption into the cells lining the small intestine, shorter fatty acids, which are water soluble, enter the blood and are transported to the liver. Larger fatty acids and monoglycerides are reassembled into triglycerides and then combined with cholesterol, phospholipids, and protein to form particles called **chylomicrons**. Chylomicrons are a type of **lipoprotein** that transports lipids from the intestines. Chylomicrons move from the intestinal cells into the **lymph**, a fluid that then carries them to the bloodstream. Chylomicrons travel in the blood, delivering triglycerides to the body cells. To enter body cells, an enzyme must first break the triglycerides into fatty acids and glycerol. What remains of the chylomicron goes to the liver.

When they reach the liver, the remnants of chylomicrons, as well as the triglycerides and cholesterol that are synthesized in the liver, are incorporated into lipoprotein particles called **very-low-density lipoproteins (VLDLs)**. VLDLs transport lipids from the liver and deliver triglycerides to body cells. As with chylomicrons, an

SEEING THE FAT YOU EAT

If a blood sample is taken from a person who has just eaten a fatty meal, his or her blood plasma will look white like milk. Plasma is the blood fluid. Between meals it is a clear, yellowish liquid. After a fatty meal the high concentration of chylomicrons formed to transport the fat makes the plasma look white and opaque. People who are having their blood lipids measured are usually asked to fast for 8 to 10 hours before the blood sample is taken. Otherwise, the blood sample will include the chylomicrons carrying the fat from their most recent meal.

enzyme breaks the triglycerides in VLDLs into fatty acids and glycerol so they can be taken up by cells. After triglycerides have been removed from the VLDLs, these particles can either be returned to the liver or transformed into lipoproteins called **low-density lipoproteins (LDLs).** LDLs deliver cholesterol to body cells. For LDLs to be taken up by cells, the LDL particle must bind to a protein on the cell membrane, which is called an LDL receptor. High levels of LDLs in the blood are associated with an increased risk for heart disease and, therefore, are thought of as "bad" cholesterol.

Cholesterol that is not used by cells can be returned to the liver by lipoproteins called **high-density lipoproteins (HDLs).** High levels of HDLs in the blood are associated with a reduction in heart disease risk, therefore HDLs are thought of as "good" cholesterol.

LIPID METABOLISM: USING AND STORING FAT

The fatty acids we consume in our diets can be used to produce ATP via cellular respiration. For this to occur, the carbon chains of the fatty acids must first be broken into 2-carbon units that form acetyl-CoA. Acetyl-CoA can then be metabolized by aerobic metabolism, the type of metabolism that requires oxygen, to generate ATP. After the body's immediate need for energy is met, remaining fatty acids can be stored as triglycerides in the **adipose tissue**. As more fat is stored, adipose tissue cells get bigger. They can increase in weight by about 50 times, and new fat cells can be made when existing cells reach their maximum size.

When the diet contains just enough calories to meet needs, the net amount of stored triglyceride in adipose tissue does not change and body weight remains constant. When fewer calories are consumed than are needed, the body releases stored triglycerides to be used for fuel and weight is lost. When more calories are consumed than needed, the excess calories are stored as triglycerides in the adipose tissue and body weight increases. If the excess calories come from fat, the fatty acids are transported directly to the adipose tissue for storage. Excess calories that come from carbohydrates or proteins must first go to the liver where they can be used to synthesize fatty acids, which are then assembled into triglycerides and delivered to the adipose tissue for storage.

LIPIDS AND HEART DISEASE

Diets that are high in saturated fat, cholesterol, and trans fat may increase the risk of developing heart disease, in particular, **atherosclerosis**. Atherosclerosis is a type of heart disease in which a fatty substance called **plaque** builds up in **arteries**. Plaque causes an artery to narrow and lose its elasticity (Figure 4.4). The buildup of plaque can become so great that it completely blocks the artery, or the plaque can rupture and cause a blood clot to form. The blood clots can block the artery at that spot or break loose and block a smaller artery elsewhere. When blood flow is blocked the cells that the artery supplies with blood are starved for oxygen and die. If an artery in the heart is blocked, heart muscle cells die, resulting in a heart attack, or **myocardial infarction**. If the blood flow to the brain becomes blocked, brain cells die and a stroke results.

There are many factors that affect the risk of developing atherosclerosis. The risk increases as people get older and increases with high blood pressure, diabetes, obesity, high blood LDL cholesterol,

HIGH BLOOD PRESSURE IS A FORM OF HEART DISEASE

High blood pressure or **hypertension** is a type of **cardiovascular disease**. It has been called the silent killer because it has no symptoms, but having hypertension increases the risk of atherosclerosis, kidney disease, and stroke. It is a serious public health problem in the United States: About 25% of adult Americans and more than half of those over age 60 years have hypertension. And about 30% of the Americans with hypertension don't know they have it.

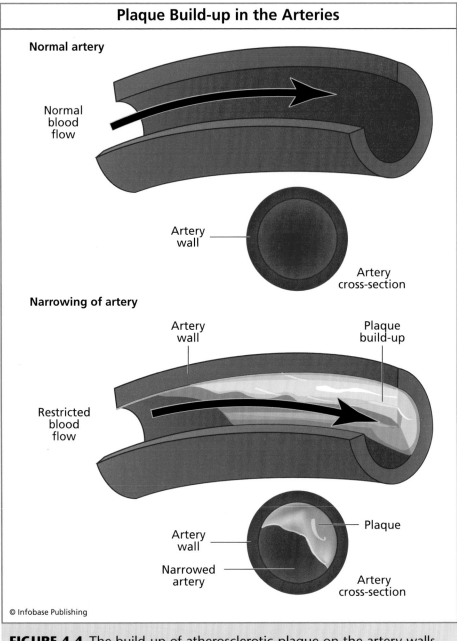

Plaque Build-up in the Arteries

Normal artery

Normal blood flow

Artery wall

Artery cross-section

Narrowing of artery

Artery wall

Plaque build-up

Restricted blood flow

Plaque

Artery wall

Narrowed artery

Artery cross-section

© Infobase Publishing

FIGURE 4.4 The build-up of atherosclerotic plaque on the artery walls narrows the artery and impedes blood flow.

and low blood HDL cholesterol (Table 4.1). Lifestyle factors such as lack of exercise, stress, cigarette smoking, and a diet high in saturated fat, trans fat, and cholesterol also increase risk. On the other hand, regular exercise decreases risk by promoting the maintenance of a healthy body weight, reducing the risk of diabetes, increasing HDL cholesterol, and reducing blood pressure.

A number of dietary factors help lower the risk of atherosclerosis. Diets that are high in omega-3 fatty acids reduce **LDL** cholesterol levels and help to prevent the growth of atherosclerotic plaque by affecting blood clotting, blood pressure, and immune function. Diets that are high in monounsaturated fats, such as those consumed in Mediterranean countries where olive oil is commonly used, also reduce LDL cholesterol and keep HDL levels high. Diets high in plant foods are associated with a lower risk of heart disease. This may be due to the higher amounts fiber, antioxidants, and phytochemicals contained in these diets. Moderate alcohol consumption has also been shown to lower risk by reducing stress, raising HDL cholesterol levels, and reducing blood clotting.

HOW MUCH AND WHAT KIND OF FAT DO WE NEED?

There are recommendations about both the types and amounts of lipids that should be included in the diet. To prevent lipid deficiencies, a small proportion of lipids needs to come from essential fatty acids; the DRIs include specific recommendations for these amounts. To meet calorie needs and balance the amounts of carbohydrate, protein, and fat in our diets, the DRIs recommend that American adults consume between 20% and 35% of their calories as fat. To meet the needs for growth, the recommended ranges of fat intake are higher for children: 30 to 40% of calories for 1- to 3-year-old children and 25 to 35% of calories for 3- to 18-year-olds.

TABLE 4.1 FACTORS THAT AFFECT HEART DISEASE RISK

Age: Risk increases as people age.

Sex: Males have a higher risk until age 65, after which risks do not differ between the sexes.

Disease factors:

Diabetes: fasting blood sugar 126 mg/100 mL or greater

High blood pressure: greater than 140/90

Obesity: body mass index greater than 27 kg/m^2

High blood lipid levels:

	Low Risk	Moderate Risk	High Risk
Total cholesterol (mg/100 mL)	< 200	200–239	≥ 240
LDL cholesterol (mg/100 mL)	< 100	100–159	≥ 160
HDL (mg/100 mL)	≥ 60	40–59	< 40

Lifestyle:

Risk is increased by:

- Cigarette smoking
- Stress
- Sedentary lifestyle

Risk is decreased by:

- Regular exercise

Diet:

Risk is increased by:

- High saturated fat intake
- High cholesterol intake
- High intake of trans fat

(continues)

TABLE 4.1 FACTORS THAT AFFECT HEART DISEASE RISK *(continued)*

Risk is decreased by:
- High intakes of monounsaturated fatty acids
- High intakes of polyunsaturated fatty acids with a healthy ratio of omega-3 and omega-6 fatty acids
- High-fiber intake
- High intake of whole grains, fruits, and vegetables

The current amount of fat in the typical American diet is within the range recommended, but Americans often don't consume the right types of fat. The DRIs recommend that cholesterol, saturated fat, and trans fat intake be kept to a minimum to decrease the risk of heart disease. To help people choose healthy fats and avoid unhealthy ones, the Dietary Guidelines and MyPyramid recommend that they choose liquid oils and avoid solid fats. Liquid oils such as olive oil, canola oil, and soybean oil are usually sources of monounsaturated and polyunsaturated fats. Solid fats, such as butter, lard, and shortening are generally higher in saturated fat, cholesterol, or trans fat. These guidelines also recommend that we consume healthy high-fat foods such as nuts, which are high in monounsaturated fats and omega-3 fatty acids and fish, which are high in omega-3 fatty acids.

REVIEW

Lipids, which are commonly called fats, include fatty acids, triglycerides, phospholipids, and sterols. Most of the fat in our diets and in our bodies is triglycerides, which consist of three fatty acids attached to a molecule of glycerol. Fatty acids can be either saturated or unsaturated. Saturated fats are most abundant in animal foods. Diets high in saturated fats are associated with an increased risk of heart disease. Unsaturated fats include mono-

and polyunsaturated fats. They are found primarily in plant foods and diets that are high in these fats reduce the risk of heart disease. Trans fats are a type of unsaturated fat produced during a process called hydrogenation that is used to make margarine from vegetable oils. Diets high in trans fat increase the risk of heart disease. Phospholipids act as emulsifiers in foods. In our

HOW MUCH FAT IS IN YOUR DIET?

The DRIs recommend that adults consume between 20% and 35% of their energy from fat, but how do you know the percentage of fat in your diet? To find out, you need to know how many calories and how many grams of fat you eat each day. You can get this information by using a diet analysis computer program or food composition tables. Knowing that fat provides 9 calories per gram allows you to do the following calculation:

- Multiply the grams of fat by 9 calories per gram

    Grams fat x 9 calories per gram = calories from fat

- Divide calories from fat by total calories in the diet and multiply by 100 to express as a percent

$$\frac{\text{Calories from fat}}{\text{Total calories}} \times 100 = \text{Percent of calories from fat}$$

For example:
If your diet contains 2,000 calories and 62 g of fat

$$62 \text{ g of fat} \times 9 \text{ cal/g} = 558 \text{ calories from fat}$$

$$\frac{558 \text{ calories from fat}}{2,000 \text{ calories}} \times 100 = 28\% \text{ of calories from fat}$$

bodies, phospholipids are an important component of cell membranes. Cholesterol is a type of sterol found only in animal foods. In the body, it is needed in cell membranes and nerve sheaths and to synthesize vitamin D, bile, and hormones. High intakes of cholesterol may increase the risk of heart disease. In the body, lipids are transported through the blood in particles called lipoproteins. Blood levels of lipoproteins affect heart disease risk: LDLs increase the risk, HDLs decrease risk. Recommendations for a healthy diet suggest that adults consume between 20% and 35% of energy from fat and limit the amount of saturated fat, trans fat, and cholesterol in their diet.

5

PROTEIN

Strength, health, and vitality—all of these attributes are associated with protein. Body builders eat protein to bulk up their muscles, fashion models eat it to make their skin glow, and manufacturers add it to shampoos to strengthen hair. What is this substance? Does it really do all these wondrous things for us?

WHAT IS PROTEIN?

The proteins that make up our muscles, skin, and hair are large molecules made of chain-like strands of smaller molecules that are called amino acids. Unlike carbohydrates and lipids, which are made of only carbon, hydrogen, and oxygen atoms, proteins also contain the element nitrogen. The nitrogen is a component of a chemical group called an amino group (NH_2) that is part of the structure of each amino acid. Amino acids also contain an acid group and a side

Polypeptides and Proteins

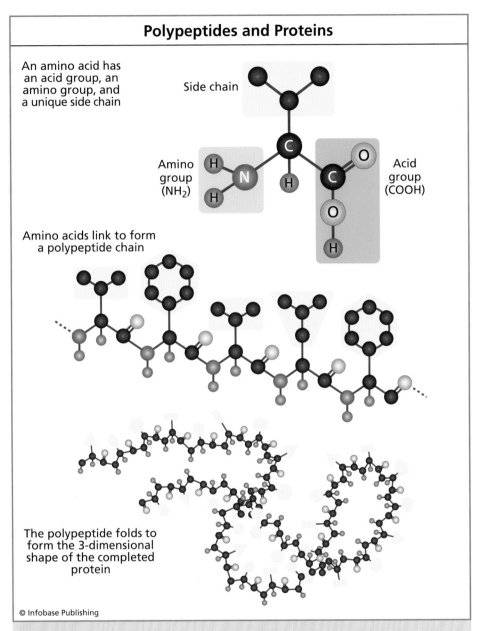

An amino acid has an acid group, an amino group, and a unique side chain

Side chain

Amino group (NH$_2$)

Acid group (COOH)

Amino acids link to form a polypeptide chain

The polypeptide folds to form the 3-dimensional shape of the completed protein

© Infobase Publishing

FIGURE 5.1 When amino acids are connected to each other, they form polypeptides, which fold to form proteins. Proteins form the structure of muscles, hair, teeth, and skin.

chain that varies in structure depending on the amino acid. Amino acids are the building blocks of proteins (Figure 5.1).

There are 20 different amino acids commonly found in proteins; they all have different side chains. Some of the amino acids found in protein can be made in the body, usually by moving the amino group from an amino acid to another molecule to form a different amino acid. Amino acids that cannot be made by the human body are called **essential amino acids** because they must be consumed in the diet. Some amino acids are considered conditionally essential; that is, they are essential only under certain conditions. For example, the amino acid tyrosine can be made in the body from the essential amino acid phenylalanine. However, if phenylalanine is deficient, tyrosine must be consumed in the diet.

To make a protein, amino acids are linked together by **peptide bonds.** For example, two amino acids linked together form a dipep-

WHAT IS A PHENYLKETONURIC?

In addition to the nutrition information listed on the label of a can of diet soda, there is a warning that reads "Phenylketonurics: Contains phenylalanine." Is this a cause for concern? What is a phenylketonuric? A phenylketonuric is someone with a genetic disease called **phenylketonuria.** Phenylketonuria (PKU) is a genetic defect in which the amino acid phenylalanine is not broken down. As a result, it accumulates in the blood and is converted into by-products called phenylketones. High levels of phenylalanine and its by-products interfere with brain development. As a result, babies and children who suffer from PKU must eat a diet low in phenylalanine in order to develop normally. Phenylalanine is usually found only in protein, but it's also found in an artificial sweetener called aspartame that is used in diet soda (there's also another amino acid in aspartame known as aspartic acid). The warning on diet soda serves to alert people with PKU that the soda, which would normally not be a source of any amino acids, contains phenylalanine.

FRIED EGGS AND SOUR MILK

When an egg is cracked and poured out of its shell into a frying pan, it hardens and changes color. This change is caused by the heat of the frying pan which is actually changing or denaturing the structure of the egg protein. This change in protein structure changes the characteristic of the egg. In this case, the egg white changes from clear and runny to hard and white. The runny yellow yolk becomes lighter in color and crumbly. Another example of this disruption in protein structure can be found when milk sours. If milk sits in the refrigerator too long, bacteria begin to take over and consume the sugar in the milk, producing acids. The acid gives the milk a sour taste and denatures the milk proteins, causing them to form solid white clumps. If the right kind of bacteria is growing in the milk, the result is yogurt.

tide; three form a tripeptide; when many amino acids are linked together, they constitute a **polypeptide**. Proteins consist of one or more polypeptide chains that fold over on themselves to form complex three-dimensional shapes. Each polypeptide contains a different number and proportion of amino acids bound together in a specific order. Variations in the number, proportion, and order of amino acids allow for an infinite number of different polypeptide and protein structures. The order of the amino acids in a polypeptide chain determines the three-dimensional shape that the final protein will have; this, in turn, affects the protein's function.

WHAT DO PROTEINS DO?

Proteins serve many different functions in the body. They provide the structure of hair and nails. They form the framework of bones into which minerals are deposited. The proteins in muscles form their structure and allow them to contract, and the proteins found in ligaments and tendons help to hold us together. Protein hormones help regulate body processes, and protein molecules that are called enzymes speed up the rate of chemical reactions in the body. Proteins are also an integral part of cell membranes where they help transport materials in and out of cells and help cells communicate with one another. Proteins in our blood help transport materials throughout the body, regulate the distribution of body water, and keep body fluids at the right acidity. Proteins produced by our immune system help protect us from disease. If necessary, body proteins can also be broken down to provide energy.

DIGESTING AND ABSORBING PROTEINS

Proteins that are consumed in the diet must be broken down in order to be absorbed into the body. Protein digestion begins in the stomach, where hydrochloric acid unfolds the polypeptide chains that make up a protein to allow the protein-digesting enzyme **pepsin** to begin breaking these large molecules into shorter polypeptides and amino acids. In the intestine, the polypeptides are broken into amino acids, dipeptides, and tripeptides by enzymes secreted by the pancreas and enzymes found on the surface of the cells lining the small intestine. The amino acids, dipeptides, and tripeptides are absorbed into the intestinal cells where dipeptides and tripeptides are broken into single amino acids by enzymes found inside the intestinal cells.

Amino acids are absorbed into the intestinal cells by several different energy-requiring transport systems. Amino acids with similar structures share the same transport system and therefore compete with each other for absorption. If there is an excess of any one of the amino acids that share a transport system, more of the excess amino acid will be absorbed and, therefore, slow the absorption of the other amino acids. For this reason, taking supplements of a single amino acid can block the absorption of others that share the same transport system.

WHAT ARE AMINO ACIDS USED FOR?

Once the amino acids from dietary protein have been absorbed, they become available to make the proteins needed by the body, to make other molecules that contain nitrogen, and to provide energy.

Making Body Proteins

To keep the body healthy, body proteins are continuously broken down and replaced with new ones. New proteins are synthesized from amino acids, some of which come from protein consumed in the diet while some come from the breakdown of old body proteins. Of the approximately 300 grams of protein synthesized by the body each day, only about 100 grams are made of amino acids that come from the diet. The other 200 grams are made from amino acids recycled from protein that is broken down in the body.

The instructions for making body proteins are contained in **deoxyribonucleic acid (DNA)**, the genetic information in the nucleus of cells. A stretch of DNA that provides the blueprint for the structure of a protein is called a **gene**. To make a protein, the information from a gene is copied into a molecule of ribonucleic acid (RNA). The RNA takes this information from the nucleus to structures located in the cell's cytoplasm that are called ribosomes. At the ribosome, the information in RNA is translated into the sequence of amino acids that makes up the protein (Figure 5.2).

Which proteins are made and when they are made is regulated. For example, if a protein is not needed, it is not made, but if the body needs a protein, the process of protein synthesis is turned on. For the process to be completed, all the amino acids in that protein must be available. If one of them is missing, protein synthesis stops until the amino acid is provided. If the missing amino acid is a nonessential amino acid, it can be made by the body. If the missing amino acid is an essential amino acid, the body must break down other body proteins to obtain it. The essential amino

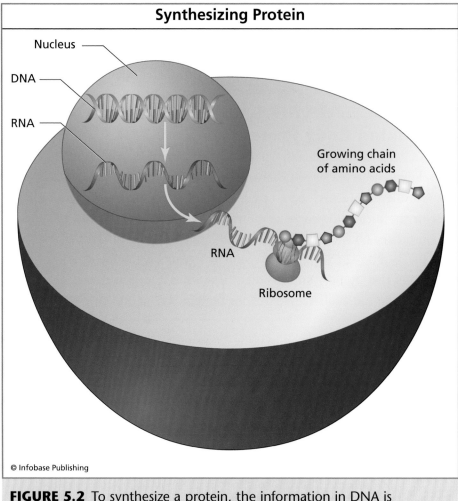

Synthesizing Protein

Nucleus

DNA

RNA

Growing chain
of amino acids

RNA

Ribosome

© Infobase Publishing

FIGURE 5.2 To synthesize a protein, the information in DNA is transcribed into a molecule of RNA. The RNA takes the information to the ribosomes in the cytoplasm of the cell, where it dictates the sequence of amino acids in a protein.

acid present in the shortest supply relative to need is called the **limiting amino acid**, because lack of this amino acid limits the ability to make the needed protein.

Making Nonprotein Molecules

Amino acids are also used to make nonprotein molecules that contain nitrogen. These include the units that make up DNA and

RNA, the high-energy molecule ATP, the skin pigment melanin, a number of **neurotransmitters**, and histamine, which causes blood vessels to dilate.

Providing Energy

Carbohydrates and fat are more efficient energy sources than protein, but when the diet provides more protein than the body needs, some of the amino acids from dietary protein can be used to provide energy. Protein is also used as an energy source when the diet does not contain enough energy to meet needs. In this situation, body proteins are broken down into amino acids to supply energy.

To be used as an energy source, the nitrogen-containing amino group must be removed from amino acids. The remaining molecule can then enter the citric acid cycle to produce ATP or be used to make glucose via gluconeogenesis. Body proteins can provide energy and glucose in times of need, such as during endurance exercise or fasting, but using them for this purpose also robs the body of functional proteins.

HOW DOES PROTEIN INTAKE AFFECT HEALTH?

Although protein deficiency is uncommon in the United States, inadequate protein is a very real concern in developing nations. Diets that lack protein are often deficient in energy as well, but a pure protein deficiency can occur when protein needs are high and the available foods are very low in protein. The term **protein-energy malnutrition (PEM)** is used to refer to conditions ranging from pure protein deficiency, known as **kwashiorkor**, to a general deficiency of calories, known as **marasmus** (Figure 5.3).

The word *kwashiorkor* means "the disease that the first child gets when the second child is born." The condition happens like this: When a new baby is born, the first child is no longer breast-fed. Instead of high-protein breast milk, he or she is fed the same starchy, high-fiber diet that adults consume. The small child is

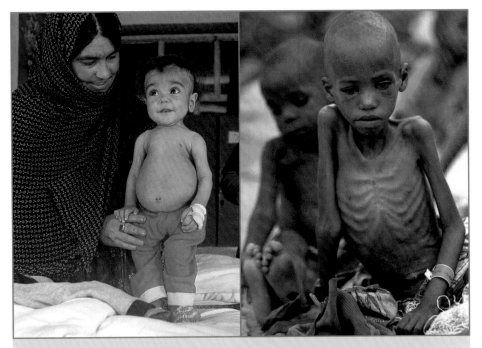

FIGURE 5.3 Protein deficiencies can cause kwashiorkor and marasmus, two diseases that often affect children in developing countries. The two-year-old Afghani child on the left has kwashiorkor, while the Rwandan child on the right suffers from marasmus. Kwashiorkor can cause fat and liquids to build up in the belly; marasmus results in stunted growth and the wasting away of fat and muscle.

unable to consume enough of this low-protein diet to meet his or her protein needs. The symptoms of kwashiorkor include reduced growth, increased susceptibility to infection, changes in hair color, dry flaking skin, and a bloated belly. Children with kwashiorkor have bloated bellies because fat accumulates in their livers and fluid accumulates in their abdomens. Although kwashiorkor is often thought of as a disease of children, it is also seen in sick adults who have high-protein needs due to infection or trauma and a low-protein intake because they are unable to eat.

The word *marasmus* means "to waste away." The lack of energy causes growth to slow or stop, body fat stores to be depleted, and muscles to shrink, making the body appear emaciated. This is the form of malnutrition that occurs with eating disorders. It has devastating effects in infants and children because adequate energy is essential for growth and brain development. It is seen in the United States in patients with cancer as well as in individuals who are starving due to an eating disorder.

An excess intake of protein has no immediate effects other than increasing fluid needs. The extra fluid is needed to excrete the additional nitrogen that is removed when amino acids are broken down. It has been suggested that the long-term consumption of diets high in protein may have a negative effect on kidney function and bone health. However, high protein diets do not appear to be a problem for people with healthy kidneys and bone health is not compromised by high protein intake as long as dietary calcium is adequate. Another concern associated with high-protein diets is that they are high in animal foods, which are high in saturated fat and cholesterol and may therefore increase the risk of heart disease.

HOW MUCH PROTEIN DO YOU NEED?

The DRIs recommend 0.8 grams of protein per kilogram of body weight per day for everyone 19 years of age or older; this is about 72 grams per day for a 200-pound man (Table 5.1). A typical American diet exceeds this, providing about 90 grams daily. This amount of protein, however, is within the recommended range of protein intake: 10 to 35% of calories.

Protein needs per kilogram of body weight are higher for children, teens, and pregnant women because additional protein is needed for growth. Lactation also increases the body's protein demand because the milk produced and secreted is high in protein. Extreme stresses on the body, such as infections, fevers, burns, and surgery, increase protein losses and, therefore, increase dietary needs. Endurance and strength sports may also increase protein needs. In endurance events such as marathons, protein is used for energy and to maintain blood glucose, so athletes involved in these

TABLE 5.1 CALCULATING PROTEIN NEEDS

To determine protein requirement:
- Determine body weight. If weight is measured in pounds, convert it to kilograms by dividing by 2.2 lbs/kg:

  weight in lbs ÷ 2.2 lbs/kg = weight in kg

  For example:

  150 lbs ÷ 2.2 lbs/kg = 68 kg
- Determine the grams of protein required per day. Multiply weight in kg by the grams of protein per kilogram recommended (see below) for the specific gender and life-stage group.
- For example, a 23-year-old woman weighing 68 kg would require: 0.8 g/kg per day x 68 kg = 54.4 grams of protein per day.

Age (yrs)	Recommendation (g/kg/day)
0–0.5	1.52
0.5–1	1.5
1–3	1.1
4–8	0.95
9–13	0.95
14–18	0.85
19 and older	0.8

activities may benefit from 1.2 to 1.4 grams of protein per kilogram per day. Strength athletes who require amino acids to synthesize new muscle proteins may benefit from 1.2 to 1.7 grams per kilogram per day. This amount, however, is not much more than the amount contained in the diets of typical American athletes. For example, a 190-pound man who consumes 3,000 calories, 18% of which comes from protein, consumes 135 grams, or 1.6 grams of protein per kilogram of body weight. If the diet is adequate in energy, enough protein can easily be obtained from the diet without protein or amino acid supplements.

TABLE 5.2 **TYPES OF VEGETARIAN DIETS**	
Diet	**What it excludes**
Semi-vegetarian	Red meat (but may include fish and poultry, as well as dairy products and eggs)
Pescetarian	All animal flesh (except for fish)
Lacto-ovo vegetarian	All animal flesh but does allow eggs and dairy products
Lacto vegetarian	All animal flesh and eggs but allows dairy products
Vegan	All food of animal origin

VEGETARIAN DIETS

When we think of protein, we usually think of animal foods such as beef, chicken, milk, and cheese. However, plant foods such as soybeans, sunflower seeds, almonds, and rice also provide protein. Much of the world survives primarily on plant proteins—mostly out of necessity because animal foods are typically more expensive and less available. In affluent societies where animal foods are available, some people may still choose to consume only plant proteins for health, religious, ethical, or environmental reasons. The strictest of these vegetarian diets eliminates all animal foods—these are called **vegan** diets. Other vegetarian diets allow some animal foods. For example, lacto-ovo vegetarians eat no animal flesh but do eat eggs and dairy products (Table 5.2).

Protein Complementation

Generally, the proteins in animal foods provide a mixture of amino acids that is closer to what the body needs than plant proteins do. Therefore, animal proteins are said to be of higher **protein quality** than plant proteins. Plant proteins are limited in one or more essential amino acids. Vegetarians are able to meet their

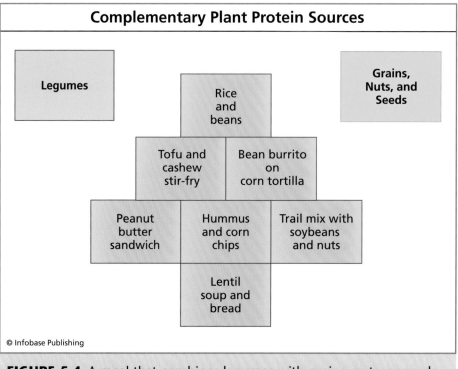

Complementary Plant Protein Sources

Legumes

Grains, Nuts, and Seeds

Rice and beans

Tofu and cashew stir-fry

Bean burrito on corn tortilla

Peanut butter sandwich

Hummus and corn chips

Trail mix with soybeans and nuts

Lentil soup and bread

© Infobase Publishing

FIGURE 5.4 A meal that combines legumes with grains, nuts, or seeds provides more complete protein than either of these plant protein sources provides alone.

protein needs by consuming a mix of plant proteins that provides all of the amino acids needed to build body proteins. This is the principle of **protein complementation**—combining foods containing proteins with different limiting amino acids in order to improve the protein quality of the diet as a whole.

The amino acids that are most often limited in plant proteins are lysine, methionine, cysteine, and tryptophan. As a general rule, legumes such as chickpeas, black beans, peanuts, and lentils are deficient in methionine and cysteine but high in lysine. Grains, nuts, and seeds are deficient in lysine but high in methionine and cysteine. Corn is deficient in lysine and tryptophan but is a good source of methionine. By combining plant proteins with complementary amino acid patterns, all essential amino acid requirements can be met (Figure 5.4). Although it is not necessary to consume complementary proteins at each meal, the entire day's diet should include proteins from a variety of plant sources in order to satisfy the daily need for amino acids.

Pros and Cons of Vegetarian Diets

Vegetarian diets can be a healthy alternative to the typical meat-based diet. Because they limit animal foods, they are lower in saturated fat and cholesterol and because they tend to be higher in grains, legumes, vegetables, and fruits, they are higher in fiber, certain vitamins and minerals, and phytochemicals. Vegetarians have been shown to have lower risks for obesity, diabetes, cardio-vascular disease, high blood pressure, and some types of cancer.

However, despite their health benefits, vegetarian diets can be deficient in certain vitamins and minerals. Diets that exclude red meat may be low in iron and zinc because red meats are the best sources of these minerals. Vegan diets, which exclude dairy prod-ucts, may be deficient in calcium and vitamin D. Vegan diets may also be deficient in vitamin B_{12} because this vitamin is only found in animal products, unless it is added by fortification. Obtaining enough omega-3 fatty acids, particularly DHA and EPA, is also a concern for vegetarians. Nutrient deficiencies are a particular concern if vegetarian diets are consumed by those with increased needs such as small children or pregnant women, but vitamin B_{12} deficiency is a concern for anyone eating a vegan diet.

Choosing a Healthy Vegetarian Diet

Well-planned vegetarian diets, including vegan diets, can meet the nutrient needs at all stages of life. One way to plan a vegetar-ian diet is to modify the selections from MyPyramid. The food choices and recommended number of servings from the grains, vegetables, and fruits groups are the same for vegetarians and non-vegetarians. Including one cup of dark green leafy vegetables daily will help vegetarians meet their iron and calcium needs. The meat and beans group and the milk group include foods of animal origin. Vegetarians who consume eggs and milk can still choose

DOES GOING GREEN MEAN GOING VEGETARIAN?

One of the reasons people choose to adopt vegetarian diets is concern about the environment. It takes more energy and resources to raise animals than it does to grow plants. For every 100 calories of plant material a cow eats, only 10 calories are stored in the cow and can be consumed by humans. In the United States, a pound of pork provides 1,000 to 2,000 calories in the diet and costs 14,000 calories to produce. The environmental costs of livestock production are also high, accounting for over 8% of global water use and 70% of agricultural land use. Livestock is responsible for 18% of agricultural green house gas emissions, more than comes from all the cars in the world. Yet, although it is more efficient to take animals out of this equation, that solution is not necessarily the best one.

If animals are used sparingly and wisely, they will cause less environmental damage and can add to the food supply, rather than waste the grain that humans might eat. The natural ecosystems of the Earth include both plants and animals. Animals can live on land that will not support crops and eat plants that will not nourish humans. Eliminating animal products entirely would reduce both the variety of food and the nutrient content of the human diet. A better solution is to develop sustainable agricultural systems in which cattle and sheep would eat only from grazing lands that are unsuitable for growing crops, rather than be fed grains that can be consumed by humans. Both plants and animals are essential for a diversified ecosystem, and both plant and animal foods make valuable contributions to the human diet.

these foods. Those who do not include any animal foods can substitute soymilk or other milk substitutes fortified with calcium and vitamin D for dairy foods and choose dry beans, nuts, and seeds from the meat and beans group. To obtain adequate vitamin B_{12}, vegans must take B_{12} supplements or use products fortified with vitamin B_{12}. Obtaining plenty of omega-3 fatty acids from vegetable oils, nuts, and flax seeds will help ensure that adequate amounts of DHA and EPA can be synthesized.

REVIEW

Protein in the diet provides the building blocks for body proteins. Proteins are made of chain-like strands of amino acids. Some amino acids are dietary essentials and some can be made in the body. The order and number of amino acids is unique to each protein and determines the final structure of the protein, which in turn determines its function. DNA in the nucleus of body cells contains the information needed to synthesize proteins from amino acids. Body proteins provide structure and also serve regulatory roles as enzymes, hormones, and molecules that transport substances into and out of cells and throughout the body. They play a role in the immune system, in muscle contraction, and in fluid and acid balance. Protein can also be metabolized to provide energy. Amino acids are also needed to synthesize a number of small, nitrogen-containing molecules. The typical American diet provides plenty of protein for most people. A diet that is deficient in protein leads to protein-energy malnutrition, which includes the conditions known as kwashiorkor and marasmus, both of which are significant health problems in developing countries. Protein in the diet is found in both animal and plant foods. The protein in animal foods provides a mix of amino acids that better meets human needs and is therefore said to be high-quality protein. Combining lower-quality protein from different plant sources can ensure that the protein quality of a vegetarian diet is sufficient to meet protein needs. Vegetarian diets may, however, be low in calcium, vitamin D, iron, zinc, or vitamin B_{12}. Vegetarians can choose a healthy diet by modifying their selections from MyPyramid.

6

WATER

Water—it's the elixir of life. Without water, a person cannot survive for more than about four days. The water molecule is made up of only one oxygen and two hydrogen atoms, but gram for gram, humans need more water than they do carbohydrates, fat, or protein. A lack of water will cause health symptoms faster than a lack of any other nutrient. Even minor changes in the amount and distribution of body water can be life-threatening. For example, days, and even weeks, without taking in some vitamins and minerals will not cause deficiency symptoms, but an hour of exercise in hot, humid weather can lead to nausea, dizziness, weakness, and other symptoms that are due to lack of water. If the water that's lost during exercise is not replaced, it can be a life-threatening situation.

WHERE IN YOUR BODY IS WATER LOCATED?

Water is found in varying proportions in all the tissues of the body. Some water is found inside cells and is known as **intracellular fluid** and some is located outside cells and is known as **extracellular fluid**. About a third of the water in the body is extracellular fluid. About three-fourths of this is fluid lies between cells and is called **interstitial fluid** and the rest is water in blood **plasma,** lymph, and cavities, such as the inside the gastrointestinal tract, eyes, joints, and spinal cord.

Electrolytes in Body Fluids

Body water contains dissolved substances, including sodium, potassium, and chloride. These minerals are referred to as **electrolytes** because when dissolved in water they form negatively and positively charged **ions** that conduct electrical current. Most of the sodium and chloride in the body is found in extracellular fluids, and most of the potassium is found inside cells. Electrolytes help regulate the distribution of water throughout the body.

Water Moves by Osmosis

Water can move freely across cell membranes to travel between the different body compartments. **Osmosis** is the movement of water across a membrane from an area with a low concentration of dissolved substances to an area with a high concentration of dissolved substances (Figure 6.1). Therefore, it is the concentrations of dissolved substances such as sodium, chloride, and potassium (as well as many other molecules) that determine the distribution of water among the various compartments. For example, if the concentration of sodium in the blood is high, water from the interstitial fluid is drawn into the blood and dilutes the sodium. Electrolytes help maintain fluid balance within the body by helping to keep water within a particular compartment. Electrolyte concentration is also important in regulating the total amount of body water.

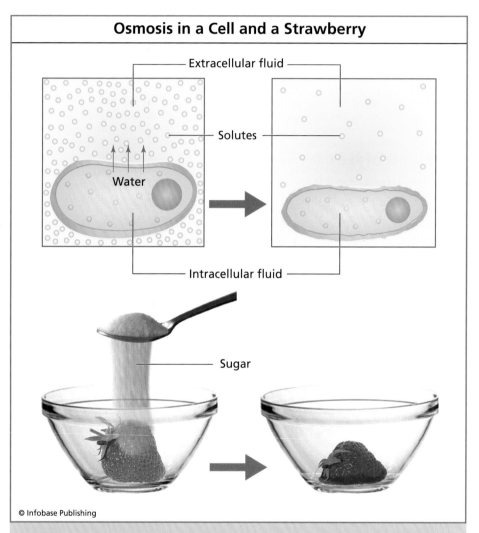

Osmosis in a Cell and a Strawberry

© Infobase Publishing

FIGURE 6.1 When the concentration of solvents in the fluid surround cell is greater than the concentration inside the cells, water will move out of the cells, causing them to shrink (*left*). This same process occurs when you sprinkle sugar on strawberries (*right*). The sugar dissolves in the moisture on the surface of the strawberries and osmosis causes water to move out of the strawberries to dilute the sugar. The strawberries get smaller and softer.

WHAT DOES WATER DO?

The human body is about 60% water. This water helps transport nutrients, provides structure, is involved in chemical reactions in the body, and regulates body temperature.

Water Transports Substances

Water bathes the cells of the body and serves as a transport medium to deliver substances to cells and remove wastes. For example, blood, which is 90% water, transports oxygen, nutrients, hormones, drugs, and other substances to cells. It then carries carbon dioxide and other waste products away from the cells. Water in urine helps eliminate wastes from the body.

Water Provides Structure and Protection

Water is part of the structure of a number of molecules, including glycogen and proteins. It also makes up most of the volume of body cells. It is present in all body tissues: Muscle is about 75% water, bone is 25% water, and even adipose tissue, where fat is stored, is 20% to 35% water. Water helps protect the body by serving as a lubricant and cleanser. Watery tears moisten the eyes and wash away dirt and **saliva** keeps the mouth moist to make it easier to chew and swallow food. Water also protects the body by acting as a cushion. For example, fluids inside the eyeballs and spinal cord cushion against shock and the fluid in our joints both cushions and lubricates them as we move.

Water Is Needed for Chemical Reactions

Water plays a role in numerous chemical reactions throughout the body. Among the roles it plays is as a medium in which all of the body's metabolic reactions occur. Water is an ideal **solvent** for many substances because the two ends of the water molecule have different electrical charges—one end is positive and one end is negative. This property allows water to surround other charged molecules and disperse them. For example, table salt, which dissolves in water, consists of a positively charged sodium ion bound to a negatively charged chloride ion. When placed in water, the sodium and chloride ions move apart because the positively charged sodium ion is attracted to the negative end of the water molecule and the negatively charged chloride ion is attracted to the positive end.

Water also participates directly in a number of chemical reactions, many of which are involved in energy production. The addition of water to a large molecule can break it into two smaller ones. Likewise, the removal of a water molecule can join two molecules together. Some of the reactions in which water participates help maintain the proper level of acidity in the body, in some cases by participating directly in a chemical reaction and in other cases by helping to transport substances to the lungs or kidneys for excretion.

Water Regulates Body Temperature

The metabolic reactions that are essential for life generate heat. To maintain body temperature in the range that is compatible with health and life, this heat must be eliminated. Likewise, in a cold environment, heat must be conserved so body temperature does not drop too low.

The water in blood helps regulate body temperature by increasing or decreasing the amount of heat lost at the body surface. When body temperature starts to rise, the blood vessels in the skin dilate (meaning the opening becomes wider), which increases blood flow to the skin and allows more heat to be released into the environment. This is why your skin turns red in hot weather or during strenuous activity. In a cold environment, the opposite occurs. The blood vessels in the skin constrict, which restricts the flow of blood near the surface and conserves body heat.

The most obvious way that water helps regulate body temperature is through the evaporation of sweat. When body temperature increases, the brain triggers the sweat glands in the skin to produce sweat, which is mostly water. As the sweat evaporates from the skin, heat is lost, cooling the body.

WATER INTAKE

Water in the body comes from water in the diet—mostly as water itself and other fluids but also from solid food (Table 6.1). For example, low-fat milk is 90% water, apples are about 85% water, and roast beef is about 50% water. A small amount of water is generated inside the body by metabolism, but this is not significant in meeting body water needs.

Water is absorbed from the gastrointestinal tract by osmosis. The rate of this absorption is influnced by the volume of water and the concentration of nutrients consumed with it. Consuming a large vol-

TABLE 6.1 **THE AMOUNT OF WATER IN FOODS**

Food	Amount of water	Percent water by weight
Orange, 1 medium	114 g (4 oz)	87
Grapes, 1 cup	129 g (4.6 oz)	81
Carrots, 1 cup	108 g (3.8 oz)	88
Broccoli, 1 cup	81 g (2.9 oz)	89
Spaghetti, 1 cup	87 g (3.1 oz)	62
Whole wheat bread, 2 slices	19 g (0.7 oz)	38
Low-fat yogurt, 1 cup	208 g (7.3 oz)	85
Ice cream, 1 cup	88 g (3.1 oz)	61
Chicken breast, 85 g (3 ounces)	55 g (1.9 oz)	65
Egg, hard cooked, 1	37 g (1.3 oz)	74

ume of water increases its rate of absorption. Water consumed alone will easily move from the intestine into the blood, where the concentration of dissolved substances (**solutes**) is higher. When water is consumed with a meal, absorption slows down because the digestion of nutrients from the meal increases the concentration of solutes in the intestine. As the nutrients from the meal are absorbed and move from the intestine into the blood, the solute concentration in the intestine decreases so water then moves by osmosis into the blood (toward the area with the highest solute concentration).

About 7 cups (1.7 liters) of water enters the GI tract each day from the diet. Another 29 cups (7 L) comes from saliva and other gastrointestinal secretions. Most of this fluid is absorbed in the small intestine, but a small amount of it is also absorbed in the colon.

WATER LOSSES

Water is lost from the body in urine and feces, through evaporation from the lungs and skin, and in sweat. A typical young man who manages to avoid sweating loses about 4 quarts (3.7 L) of water daily.

Average urine output is about 4 to 8 cups (1 to 2 L) per day, but this varies depending on the amount of fluid consumed and the amount of waste to be excreted. The waste products that must be excreted in urine include **urea** and other nitrogen-containing wastes generated from protein breakdown, ketones resulting from fat breakdown, plus phosphates, sulfates, electrolytes, and other minerals. The amount of urea that must be excreted increases when dietary protein intake or body protein breakdown rises. Ketone excretion is increased when body fat is broken down, such as during weight loss. The amount of sodium that must be excreted goes up when more is consumed in the diet. In all of these cases, the need for water increases in order to produce more urine to excrete the extra wastes.

The amount of water lost in the feces is usually small, less than a cup (100 to 200 milliliters) per day. This is remarkable, because every day about 38 cups (9 L) of fluid enter the gastrointestinal tract via food, water, and gastrointestinal secretions. Under normal conditions, more than 95% of this fluid is reabsorbed before the feces are eliminated. However, in cases of severe diarrhea, large amounts of water can be lost through the gastrointestinal tract.

Water loss due to evaporation from the skin and respiratory tract takes place continuously. These losses are referred to as **insensible losses** because the individual is unaware that they are occurring. An inactive person at room temperature loses about 4 cups (1 L) per day through insensible losses, but the amount varies depending on body size, environmental temperature and humidity, and physical activity. For example, people lose more water when the humidity is low, such as it is in the desert, than they lose on a rainy day.

Water is also lost in sweat. The amount of water lost via sweat is extremely variable depending on environmental conditions

DIARRHEA CAN BE DEADLY

Diarrhea kills about 2 million children around the world every year. It is usually caused by a bacterial or viral infection, and death is caused by dehydration. Diarrhea depletes the body of water and electrolytes. When dehydration becomes severe, it can cause collapse of blood circulation and result in death. Children are more likely than adults to die from diarrhea because they become dehydrated more quickly. To restore health when a child has diarrhea, the lost fluid must be replaced. Plain water is not the best choice because it replaces only the water and not the electrolytes. Mixtures of sugar, electrolytes, and water, called Oral Rehydration Solutions (ORS), will replace the lost water and electrolytes in the right proportions. The sugar contained in ORS enables the intestine to absorb the fluid and electrolytes more efficiently. Treatment with ORS alone is effective for 90 to 95% of patients who suffer from acute watery diarrhea. Since the World Health Organization (WHO) adopted ORS in 1978 as its primary tool to fight diarrhea, the mortality rate for children suffering from acute diarrhea has been cut by more than half.

(temperature, humidity, wind speed, radiant heat), clothing, exercise intensity, level of physical training, and the degree to which exercisers are acclimatized to their particular environment. Sweat rate increases as exercise intensity builds and as the environment becomes hotter and more humid. An individual doing light work at a temperature of about 84°F (29°C) will lose about 8.5 to 12.5 cups (2 to 3 L) of sweat per day. Strenuous exercise in a hot environment can cause water losses in sweat to be as high as 8.5 to 17 cups (2 to 4 L) in an hour. Clothing that allows sweat to evaporate will help keep the body cool and will decrease sweat losses.

BALANCING WATER IN WITH WATER OUT

Water cannot be stored in the body. Therefore, for the body to maintain adequate water, intake and excretion must balance. Water intake is stimulated by thirst but is not precisely regulated. Water loss is more precisely regulated by the kidneys, which can increase or decrease urinary losses.

Thirst

How do you know when you need water? The need to consume water or other fluids is signaled by the sensation of thirst. Thirst is triggered both by sensations in the mouth and signals from the brain. When you need water, your mouth becomes dry because less water is available to produce saliva. When body water levels drop, the thirst center in the brain senses a decrease in the amount of water in blood and an increase in the concentration of dissolved substances in the blood. Together, the feeling of a dry mouth and signals from the brain cause the sensation of thirst and motivate us to drink.

Thirst is not a perfect regulator of water intake, however. Feeling thirsty does not mean that you will take a drink. Also, the sensation of thirst often lags behind the need for water. For example, athletes exercising in hot weather lose water rapidly but do not experience intense thirst until they have lost so much body water that their physical performance is compromised.

Because people cannot and do not always respond to thirst, water loss from the body is regulated by the kidneys to prevent dehydration.

How Kidneys Regulate Water Excretion

The kidneys serve as a filtering system that regulates the amount of water and dissolved substances retained in the blood and excreted in the urine. As blood flows through the kidneys, water and small molecules are filtered out. Some of the water and molecules are reabsorbed into the blood and the rest are excreted in the urine. The amount of water and electrolytes that are reabsorbed depends on conditions in the body. There are two hormonal systems that regulate fluid balance.

One hormonal system that regulates water balance responds to changes in the concentration of solutes in the blood (Figure 6.2). When the concentration of solutes is high, the pituitary gland secretes **antidiuretic hormone (ADH)**. This hormone signals the kidneys to reabsorb water and reduce the amount lost in the urine. The reabsorbed water is then returned to the blood where it prevents the solute concentration from continuing to increase. When the solute concentration in the blood is low, ADH levels decrease, so less water is reabsorbed and more is excreted in the urine, which allows blood solute concentration to increase to normal.

The other system that regulates the amount of water in the body is activated by changes in blood pressure and relies on the ability of the kidneys to conserve sodium. Because water follows sodium by osmosis, changes in the amount of sodium retained or excreted result in changes in the amount of body water. Sodium is the primary determinant of extracellular fluid volume. When the concentration of sodium in the blood decreases, water moves out of the blood, causing a decrease in blood volume. A decrease in blood volume can cause a decrease in blood pressure. When blood pressure decreases, the kidneys release the enzyme **renin**, beginning a series of reactions that leads to the production of **angiotensin II**. Angiotensin II increases blood pressure both by causing the blood vessel walls to constrict and by stimulating the release of the hormone **aldosterone**, which acts on the kidneys

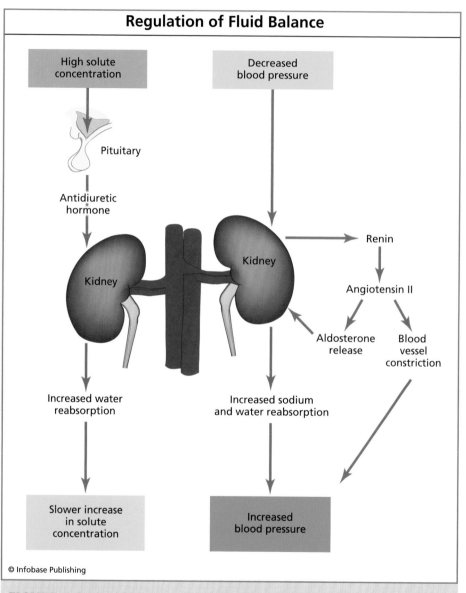

Regulation of Fluid Balance

High solute concentration

Decreased blood pressure

Pituitary

Antidiuretic hormone

Kidney

Kidney

Renin

Angiotensin II

Aldosterone release

Blood vessel constriction

Increased water reabsorption

Increased sodium and water reabsorption

Slower increase in solute concentration

Increased blood pressure

© Infobase Publishing

FIGURE 6.2 Fluid balance is regulated by antidiuretic hormone and the renin-angiotensin system, which triggers the release of the hormone aldosterone. When the body senses changes in its overall water level, it uses these systems to keep its fluids in balance.

to increase sodium reabsorption. Water follows the reabsorbed sodium, and is returned to the blood. As blood pressure returns to normal, it inhibits the release of renin and aldosterone so that blood pressure does not continue to rise.

DEHYDRATION: TOO LITTLE BODY WATER

When water losses exceed water intake, **dehydration** results. Dehydration severe enough to cause clinical symptoms can occur more rapidly than any other nutrient deficiency. Likewise, health can be restored in a matter of minutes or hours when fluid is replaced.

Early symptoms of dehydration include headache, fatigue, loss of appetite, dry eyes and mouth, and concentrated urine, which is dark in color (Figure 6.3). Even mild dehydration—a body water loss of 2% to 3% of body weight—can impair physical and cognitive performance. When 3% or more of body weight is lost as water, there can be significant reductions in the amount of blood pumped by the heart. This reduces the ability to deliver oxygen and nutrients to cells and remove waste products. As blood volume decreases, it also reduces blood flow to the skin and the production of sweat, which limits the body's ability to sweat and cool itself. Body temperature then increases and, with it, the risk of various heat-related illnesses, such as heat exhaustion and heat stroke. As water losses increase, a proportionately greater percentage of the water is lost from intracellular spaces. This water is needed to maintain metabolic functions. A loss of 5% of body weight as water can cause nausea and difficulty concentrating. When water loss approaches 7% of body weight, confusion and disorientation may occur. A loss of about 10% to 20% can result in death.

Infants, the elderly, and athletes are at risk of dehydration. Infants are at risk because their kidneys are inefficient at concentrating urine and their evaporative losses are proportionally greater because body surface area relative to body weight is much greater than in adults. In addition, infants cannot ask for

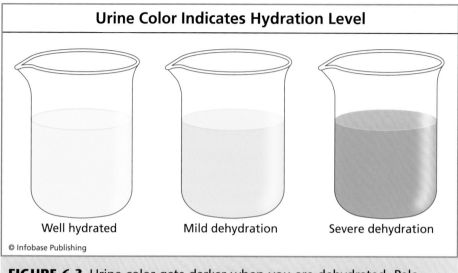

FIGURE 6.3 Urine color gets darker when you are dehydrated. Pale yellow urine indicates that you are drinking enough. The darker the urine color is, the greater the level of dehydration.

a drink when they are thirsty. Elderly people are at risk because their sense of thirst is diminished and their kidneys are less efficient at concentrating urine. Athletes are at risk because of the large amount of water they lose in sweat with strenuous exercise. Staying well hydrated is particularly important during exercise because a decrease in body water causes a decline in athletic performance.

CAN PEOPLE DRINK TOO MUCH WATER?

Too much water, or **water intoxication**, can occur either because there is too much water in the body or because there is too little sodium, which is a condition called **hyponatremia**. This can occur as a result of illness, improper administration of intravenous fluids, or from drinking too much plain water when excessive amounts of sodium have been lost in sweat. For example, hyponatremia can occur if an athlete loses large amounts of water and sodium in sweat, but drinks plain water to rehydrate. This causes the sodium that remains in blood to be diluted, making the amount of water too great for the amount of sodium. This is analogous to taking a full glass of salt water, dumping out half, and replacing what was poured out with plain water. The sodium in the glass is now diluted. It is also possible to develop hyponatremia even when salt losses from sweating are not excessive. This can occur when athletes drink too much water, which dilutes the sodium in their systems. It is the concentration of sodium that is important, not the absolute amount.

HOW MUCH SHOULD PEOPLE DRINK DURING EXERCISE?

Before Exercise:
- Begin exercise well hydrated by consuming generous amounts of fluid in the 24 hours before exercise.
- Consume about 2 cups (0.5 L) of fluid four hours before exercise.

During Exercise:
- Consume at least 6 to 12 ounces (0.2–0.4 L) of fluid every 15 to 20 minutes.
- For exercise lasting 60 minutes or less, plain water is adequate for fluid replacement.
- For exercise lasting longer than 60 minutes, a fluid containing carbohydrates and electrolytes may improve endurance and protect health.

After Exercise:
- Begin fluid replacement immediately after exercise
- Consume 2 to 3 cups (0.5 to 0.7 L) of fluid for each pound of weight lost.

A low concentration of sodium in the blood causes a number of problems. Solutes in the blood help hold fluid in the blood vessels. As sodium concentration drops, fluid leaves the bloodstream by osmosis and accumulates in the tissues, causing them to swell. Fluid accumulation in the lungs interferes with gas exchange and fluid accumulation in the brain causes disorientation, seizure, coma, and death. The early symptoms of hyponatremia may be similar to dehydration: nausea, muscle cramps, disorientation, slurred speech, and confusion. Drinking water alone will make the problem worse and can result in seizure, coma, or death.

DON'T DILUTE

When the body sweats, it loses sodium as well as water. Athletes can lose 0.9 to 1.4 grams of sodium per liter of sweat. It is not unusual for college football players to lose a liter of sweat per hour. These individuals may sweat away 3 or 4 grams of sodium during a three-hour practice. When the fluid lost in sweat is replaced with plain water, the sodium in the blood is diluted causing hyponatremia, an abnormally low concentration of sodium in the blood. Because the right balance of sodium is needed for nerves to fire and muscles to contract, this imbalance can be dangerous. It was once thought that hyponatremia was a rare occurrence, but it turns out to be more common than realized. In the 2002 Boston Marathon, 13% of runners tested had hyponatremia and 0.6% had serum sodium concentrations low enough for this condition to be considered critical. People who exercise for more than an hour should be sure to include electrolytes in their beverage. They can use a sports drink or make their own by mixing 4 teaspoons of sugar and 1/4 teaspoon of salt in a cup (0.25 L) of water. It can be flavored with a teaspoon of lemon juice.

HOW MUCH WATER DOES THE BODY NEED?

The recommendation for total water intake is about 11 cups (2.7 L) per day for women and 15 cups (3.7 L) per day for men. This amount does not all need to be consumed as water; other fluids such as juice, milk, and lemonade can also meet water needs. Water and other beverages account for about 80% of adult fluid intake. The other 20% comes from water in foods. Beverages that contain caffeine, such as coffee, tea, and caffeinated soda, provide fluid, but caffeine is a diuretic—a substance that increases water loss in the urine. In general, caffeine-containing beverages only increase water loss for a short period, so they do contribute to fluid needs over the course of the day.

Water needs can be increased above the basic recommendation by variations in activity, environment, and diet. Exercise increases water needs because it increases the amount of water lost through evaporation and sweat. Athletes can estimate their water loss by weighing themselves before and after exercise. To restore fluid balance, 2 to 3 cups (0.5 to 0.7 L) of fluid should be consumed for every pound of weight lost. A dry environment also increases water needs because more water is lost to the environment from evaporation from the skin and lungs. Low-calorie diets can also increase water needs because extra urine is produced in order to excrete ketones produced by fat breakdown. Water needs are also increased by high-protein and high-salt diets because more water is excreted in the urine to eliminate the urea from protein breakdown and the extra salt, respectively. High-fiber diets also increase water needs because the fiber increases the amount of water lost in the feces.

Water needs are higher at certain life stages. As discussed above, needs are proportionately higher during infancy because the infant's kidneys cannot concentrate urine as efficiently as adult kidneys, and they lose proportionately more water through evaporation because their surface area is large relative to body weight. An intake of 3 cups (0.7 L) per day for a six-month-old infant is recommended. Water needs are also higher for pregnant women to allow for the increase in maternal blood volume, the production of amniotic fluid, and the needs of the fetus. During lactation, fluid needs are increased because the fluid secreted in milk, about 3 cups (0.7 L) per day, must be restored by the mother's fluid intake.

REVIEW

Water is an essential nutrient. In the body, it is distributed between intracellular and extracellular compartments and moves between these by osmosis. Water transports nutrients and other substances; provides structure and protection; is needed for numerous chemical reactions; and is extremely important in the regulation of body temperature. Water is consumed in beverages and food and small amounts are produced by metabolism in the body. Water is excreted in the urine and feces and lost in sweat and through evaporation from the skin and lungs. Water cannot be stored in the body, so the intake must equal the output to maintain hydration. Water is consumed in response to thirst, but water balance is primarily regulated by the kidneys. If body water is low, antidiuretic hormone causes a reduction in urine output and other hormones cause the kidneys to retain sodium, thereby increasing water retention. A reduction in body water can have dire consequences for health. Mild dehydration can result in headache, fatigue, loss of appetite, and concentrated dark-colored urine. Severe dehydration can interfere with the function of the circulatory system and the ability of the body to cool itself and it can be fatal. Serious health problems can also occur if there is too much water relative to the amount of sodium in the blood. Water needs are increased by exercise and by hot, humid, or dry environments. Water requirements are proportionally higher in infants than in adults, and are increased in pregnant and lactating women.

7

VITAMINS

any people think of vitamins as a source of energy for our bodies. But the truth is that vitamins don't provide energy. Yet they do play a role in using the energy provided by carbohydrates, fat, and protein. This is because a number of vitamins are needed to regulate the reactions that produce ATP, the high-energy molecule that helps keep the body alive and moving. In addition to this role, vitamins are involved in a multitude of other body processes, from bone formation and vision to immune function and antioxidant protection.

SOME VITAMINS DISSOLVE IN WATER, SOME DISSOLVE IN FAT

Vitamins, by definition, are small **organic** compounds that are essential in small amounts in the diet to promote and regulate body processes. When the diet is lacking a particular vitamin, deficiency symptoms will develop. These symptoms are relieved when the vitamin is added back to the diet. Vitamins are classified based on whether they dissolve in water or fat because this property affects how they are absorbed, transported, excreted, and stored in the body.

The **water-soluble vitamins** include the B vitamins (thiamin, riboflavin, niacin, biotin, pantothenic acid, vitamin B$_6$, folate, and vitamin B$_{12}$) and vitamin C. The **fat-soluble vitamins** include vitamins A, D, E, and K. Fat-soluble vitamins are absorbed along with dietary fat and, once inside the body, they are transported with fat. Water-soluble vitamins do not need fat for absorption, but they may need transport systems that require energy or special molecules that bind to them to help them to be absorbed from the gastrointestinal tract. Some of the water-soluble vitamins must also be attached to specific proteins to be transported in the blood. With the exception of vitamin B$_{12}$, water-soluble vitamins that are consumed in excess of what the body needs are excreted in the urine. Fat-soluble vitamins, however, are not excreted in the urine but are stored in the liver and fatty tissues. Therefore, it takes longer to become deficient in vitamin B$_{12}$ and fat-soluble vitamins when they are left out of the diet.

HOW MUCH DO WE NEED?

The amount of each vitamin a person needs to remain healthy varies, depending on age, gender, size, and life stage as well as health status. DRIs have established recommendations for the amounts of each vitamin people need to prevent deficiency and promote health (Table 7.1). For some vitamins, a Tolerable Upper Intake Level (UL) has also been established; intakes above these levels increase the risk of toxicity.

THIAMIN

In Asian countries, the thiamin deficiency disease **beriberi** has been known for over 1,000 years. It became more widespread

TABLE 7.1 RECOMMENDED VITAMIN INTAKES

Vitamin	Recommended Intake Per Day for Adults	Tolerable Upper Intake Level (UL)
Thiamin	1.1–1.2 mg	Not determined
Riboflavin	1.1–1.3 mg	Not determined
Niacin	14 –16 mg NE	35 mg NE
Biotin	30 micrograms (µg)	Not determined
Pantothenic acid	5 mg	Not determined
Vitamin B_6	1.3–1.7 mg	100 mg
Folate	400 µg DFE	1000 µg DFE
Vitamin B_{12}	2.4 µg	Not determined
Vitamin C	75–90 mg	2000 mg
Vitamin A	700–900 µg	3000 µg
Vitamin D	5–15 µg	50 µg
Vitamin E	15 mg	1000 mg
Vitamin K	90–120 µg	Not determined

NE = niacin equivalents, DFE = Dietary folate equivalents

in the 1800s when the practice of polishing off the bran layer of brown rice to create polished white rice became popular. Although this created a more attractive product, it also removed the vitamin-rich portion of the grain, which increased the prevalence of beriberi. Today, the incidence of this disease in Asia is markedly decreased, partly because an improved standard of living has allowed a more varied diet and partly because of the introduction of white rice that is enriched with thiamin.

Thiamin, like the other B vitamins, is a **coenzyme.** Coenzymes are nonprotein organic molecules that act as enzyme helpers. The active coenzyme form of thiamin is needed in the body for the production of ATP from glucose and for the synthesis of acetylcholine, which is needed to transmit nerve signals. Thiamin is also needed for the metabolism of other sugars and certain amino acids and for the synthesis of ribose, a sugar that is part of the structure of RNA (ribonucleic acid).

The earliest symptoms of thiamin deficiency are depression and weakness. Other neurological symptoms include poor coordination, tingling, and paralysis. Since the brain and nervous tissue rely on glucose for energy, some beriberi symptoms may be related to the inability to use glucose completely when thiamin is deficient. Symptoms such as poor coordination, tingling, and paralysis may also be related to thiamin's role in the synthesis of acetylcholine. Beriberi can also cause cardiovascular symptoms such as a rapid heartbeat and enlarged heart, but it is not clear from the functions of thiamin why these symptoms occur.

In North America today, thiamin deficiency is rare but it does occur in alcoholics partly because alcohol decreases thiamin absorption from the gastrointestinal tract. Alcoholics are also at increased risk of deficiency because of low thiamin intake due to a poor diet. Thiamin-deficient alcoholics may develop a neurological condition known as the Wernicke-Korsakoff syndrome, which is characterized by mental confusion, psychosis, memory disturbances, and coma.

Good sources of thiamin in the diet include pork, whole grains, legumes, nuts, seeds, and organ meats (liver, kidney, and heart). Thiamin is added to enriched grains so white breads, pasta, and other enriched grain products are also good sources. The availability of thiamin may also be affected by anti-thiamin factors that are present in some foods. For example, there are enzymes present in raw shellfish and freshwater fish that destroy thiamin during storage, preparation, or passage through the gastrointestinal tract. These enzymes are not a concern if the foods are cooked as cooking destroys them. Other anti-thiamin factors that are not destroyed by cooking are found in tea, coffee, betel

BERIBERI: THE CHICKEN CONNECTION

Beriberi was a major problem in colonial Asia in the nineteenth century. It was affecting so many soldiers that, in 1886, the Dutch government sent a commission to its colony in Java (now Indonesia) to determine the cause. After several failed attempts to duplicate the disease in experimental animals, a colony of chickens suddenly developed beriberi-like symptoms and many of them died. Then, just as quickly, the surviving chickens recovered. An observant young medical officer named Christian Eijkman noted that the epidemic occurred when the chickens were fed white rice left over from a nearby hospital. The epidemic subsided when the superintendent found out that chickens were being fed expensive white rice and switched them back to brown rice. The reason brown rice prevented beriberi would not be revealed until 1912 when Polish biochemist Casamir Funk isolated a substance from rice husks that prevented beriberi.

nuts, blueberries, and red cabbage. Habitual consumption of these foods increases the risk of thiamin deficiency. No toxicity has been reported when excess thiamin is consumed from either food or supplements.

RIBOFLAVIN

Years ago, the milkman used to deliver milk in glass bottles, but not anymore. The reason for this is more than the fact that the bottles are breakable and expensive to clean. It's also because the B vitamin riboflavin is sensitive to light. Milk is one of the best sources of riboflavin in the North American diet. But if the milk is in a container that exposes it to light, much of its riboflavin will be destroyed. The most riboflavin-friendly milk containers are opaque to protect the riboflavin as well as the vitamins A and D from light. Other good dietary sources of riboflavin include meat, asparagus, broccoli, mushrooms, leafy green vegetables, and whole and enriched grains.

Riboflavin is needed to produce ATP from carbohydrates, fat, and protein. The active coenzyme forms of riboflavin function as electron carriers in the citric acid cycle and the electron transport chain. Riboflavin is also needed to convert a number of other vitamins, including folate, niacin, vitamin B_6, and vitamin K, into their active forms.

Riboflavin deficiency, called **ariboflavinosis,** is uncommon and usually occurs in conjunction with deficiencies of other B vitamins. Without riboflavin, body tissues heal poorly because new cells cannot grow to replace the damaged ones. Tissues that grow rapidly such as the skin and the linings of the eyes and mouth are most severely affected. Symptoms include inflammation of the eyes, lips, mouth, and tongue; cracking of the tissue at the corners of the mouth; increased sensitivity to light; burning, tearing, and itching of the eyes; and flaking of the skin around the nose, eyebrows, and earlobes. No adverse effects have been reported from overconsumption of riboflavin from foods or supplements.

NIACIN

In the early 1900s, the niacin deficiency disease **pellagra** was epidemic in the southeastern United States. Pellagra was prevalent because the diet among the poor people consisted of cornmeal, molasses, and fatback or salt pork, all of which are poor sources of niacin. Pellagra causes symptoms that are remembered as the three Ds: dermatitis, diarrhea, and dementia. If untreated, a fourth "D" results—death. Pellagra remained a problem in the United States until World War II (1939–1945), when economic changes led to a better diet and the federally sponsored enrichment program added niacin, thiamin, riboflavin, and iron to grains. Today, pellagra has been virtually eliminated in the United States but the disease remains common in India and parts of China and Africa.

Niacin coenzymes are electron carriers that are needed for energy metabolism and in reactions that synthesize fatty acids and cholesterol. There are two forms of niacin: nicotinic acid and nicotinamide. Both of them can be used to make active niacin coenzymes. The need for niacin in metabolism is widespread, so niacin deficiency causes major changes throughout the body.

Niacin is found primarily in meat and fish, but legumes, mushrooms, wheat bran, asparagus, peanuts, and whole and enriched grains are also good sources. Niacin can be synthesized in the body from the essential amino acid tryptophan. In a diet that is high in

THE MYSTERY OF PELLAGRA

In the early 1900s, psychiatric hospitals in the southern United States were filled with patients with the disease pellagra. At that time, no one knew what caused it. Some felt it was due to an infection or a toxin. The mystery was finally unraveled by Dr. Joseph Goldberger, who was sent by the U.S. Public Health Service to investigate the pellagra epidemic. He observed that individuals in institutions such as hospitals, orphanages, and prisons suffered from pellagra, but the staff did not. If pellagra were an infectious disease, both populations would have been equally affected. From this, Goldberger hypothesized that pellagra was due to a deficiency in the diet. To test his hypothesis, he added nutritious foods such as fresh meats, milk, and eggs to the diets of children in an orphanage. In the children who ate the healthier diet, the symptoms of pellagra disappeared, supporting Goldberger's hypothesis. In another experiment, Goldberger was able to induce pellagra in healthy prison inmates by feeding them an unhealthy diet. Despite this success, many physicians still believed pellagra to be an infectious disease. To persuade the skeptics, Goldberger and some of his colleagues injected themselves with blood from pellagra patients and swabbed their throats with nasal secretions, and swallowed capsules containing scabs from pellagra rashes. None of the volunteers got pellagra, further supporting the hypothesis that pellagra is caused by a dietary deficiency. The vitamin niacin was not identified until 1937.

protein but low in niacin, much of the needed niacin can be made from tryptophan. However, when tryptophan is needed to synthesize body proteins, it is not available to synthesize niacin.

One of the reasons pellagra was prevalent in the southern United States in the early 1900s is because the diet was based on corn. The niacin in corn is bound to other molecules, so it is not easily absorbed. In addition, corn is low in tryptophan. However, despite a corn-based diet, pellagra turns out to be uncommon in Mexico. This is partly due to the fact that the Mexican diet includes legumes, which are a good source of niacin, and partly to the fact that corn is treated with limewater during the making of tortillas, which makes the niacin more available.

Doses of 50 mg per day and greater of the nicotinamide form of niacin are used as a drug to decrease blood cholesterol levels. These amounts should only be taken when prescribed by a physician. High doses of niacin from supplements can cause toxicity symptoms including flushing, tingling in the hands and feet, a red skin rash, nausea, vomiting, diarrhea, high blood sugar levels, abnormalities in liver function, and blurred vision. The UL for adults is 35 mg per day, well below the 50 mg used to lower blood cholesterol.

BIOTIN

Biotin is a B vitamin that plays an important role in the citric acid cycle and is needed for the synthesis of glucose and the metabolism of fatty acids and amino acids. Biotin acts as a coenzyme for a group of enzymes that add the acid group COOH to molecules. Sources of biotin in the diet include liver, egg yolks, yogurt, and nuts. Raw egg whites contain a protein called **avidin** that binds with biotin, making it unavailable to the body. Cooking eggs denatures avidin so that it cannot bind with biotin. Biotin deficiency is uncommon but has been seen in people who suffer protein-energy malnutrition and in those who are being fed intravenous solutions of nutrients that are lacking biotin.

PANTOTHENIC ACID

Pantothenic acid is part of the structure of coenzyme A (CoA). Coenzyme A is needed to make acetyl-CoA, a molecule that is formed during the breakdown of carbohydrates, fatty acids, and amino acids. Pantothenic acid is also needed to form a molecule essential for the synthesis of cholesterol and fatty acids. Pantothenic acid is particularly abundant in meat, eggs, whole grains, and legumes and is found in lesser amounts in milk, vegetables, and fruits. The wide distribution of pantothenic acid in foods makes deficiency of it rare in humans; it may occur as a result of malnutrition or chronic alcoholism when many B vitamins are deficient.

VITAMIN B$_6$

The chemical term for vitamin B$_6$ is **pyridoxine**, but you may not recognize this name because this vitamin is one of only two B vitamins that we still commonly refer to by a number (vitamin B$_{12}$ is the other). Vitamin B$_6$ is noteworthy because of its importance in protein and amino acid metabolism; without vitamin B$_6$, the nonessential amino acids cannot be made in the body, the amino group cannot be removed to use the amino acid to provide energy, and the acid group cannot be removed to synthesize neurotransmitters. Vitamin B$_6$ is needed in its active coenzyme form for the activity of more than 100 enzymes involved in the metabolism of carbohydrates, fat, and protein. In addition to its role in amino acid metabolism, vitamin B$_6$ is important for the immune system and for the synthesis of **hemoglobin**, certain neurotransmitters, and lipids that are part of the myelin coating on nerves. This vitamin is also needed for the metabolism of the carbohydrate storage molecule glycogen and for the synthesis of niacin from tryptophan.

Vitamin B$_6$ is found in chicken, fish, pork, and organ meats as well as whole grains, soybeans, sunflower seeds, and some fruits and vegetables such as bananas, broccoli, and spinach. Enriched grains are a poor source because vitamin B$_6$ is lost in the milling of grains but is not added back when they are enriched.

Vitamin B_6 levels in the body can be affected by a number of drugs, including alcohol and oral contraceptives. Symptoms of vitamin B_6 deficiency include depression, headaches, confusion, numbness and tingling in the extremities, and seizures; these may be related to the role that vitamin B_6 plays in neurotransmitter synthesis and myelin formation. Anemia may occur due to vitamin B_6 deficiency because of the vitamin's role in hemoglobin synthesis.

A deficiency of vitamin B_6 may also contribute to the development of heart disease. When vitamin B_6 is not available, an amino acid called **homocysteine** accumulates in the blood. High levels of homocysteine increase the risk for heart disease. Vitamin B_{12} and folate are also needed to prevent homocysteine accumulation.

Low-dose supplements of vitamin B_6 may be beneficial in reducing the anxiety, irritability, and depression associated with premenstrual syndrome (PMS). Vitamin B_6 supplements have been found to improve immune function in older adults, but since the elderly frequently have low intakes of vitamin B_6, it is unclear whether the beneficial effects of supplements are due to an improvement in vitamin B_6 status or immune system stimulation.

Supplements of vitamin B_6 should be used with caution because vitamin B_6 is toxic. Excessive intakes of this vitamin can cause irreversible nerve damage that affects the ability to walk and causes numbness in the extremities. Intakes greater than 100 mg per day are not recommended.

FOLATE OR FOLIC ACID

Low intakes of folate during pregnancy are associated with birth defects that affect the brain and spinal cord, which are called **neural tube defects**. The connection between folate intake and neural tube defects is so strong that the U.S. government requires folic acid to be added to breads, cereals, and other grain products. Folic acid is a stable form of folate that is used in fortified foods and supplements. Since 1998, when grain products were first fortified, the incidence of neural tube defects in the United States has decreased by about 25%; a similar fortification program in Canada has resulted in a decrease of almost 50%.

In the body, the B vitamin folate is needed for the synthesis of DNA and the metabolism of some amino acids. Because a cell must synthesize DNA in order to divide, folate is particularly important when cells are dividing rapidly. A folate deficiency causes a form of anemia called **macrocytic** or **megaloblastic anemia**, which is characterized by the formation of large red blood cells. This occurs because the developing red blood cells cannot duplicate their DNA; they therefore grow bigger, but they cannot

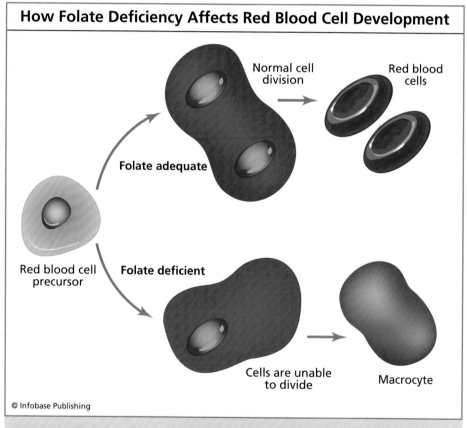

How Folate Deficiency Affects Red Blood Cell Development

Normal cell division

Red blood cells

Folate adequate

Red blood cell precursor

Folate deficient

Cells are unable to divide

Macrocyte

© Infobase Publishing

FIGURE 7.1 When folate is deficient, DNA cannot replicate so developing red blood cells are not able to divide. Instead, they grow bigger, forming megaloblasts and macrocytes.

divide (Figure 7.1). In addition to anemia, folate deficiency causes poor growth, abnormalities in nerve development and function, diarrhea, and inflammation of the tongue.

Low intakes of folate are also associated with an increased risk of heart disease, cancer, and birth defects. The connection between low intakes of folate and heart disease is the amino acid homocysteine. When folate intake is low, homocysteine can build up in the blood, increasing the risk of heart disease. Low folate intake also increases the risk of colon cancer and possibly cancers of the uterus, cervix, lung, stomach, and esophagus. The cancer risk associated with a low folate diet is greatly increased by alcohol consumption.

A low intake of folate in early pregnancy increases the risk of neural tube defects in the fetus. Although low folate is not the only cause of neural tube defects, supplemental folic acid, taken before and during early pregnancy, has been associated with a reduced incidence of these birth defects. Because of this, it is recommended that women who are capable of becoming pregnant consume folic acid from fortified foods or supplements in addition to the folate contained in a balanced diet. Dietary sources of folate include fortified foods such as breakfast cereals and other enriched grains, and natural sources such as oranges, asparagus, corn, snap beans, mustard greens, broccoli, liver, legumes, and some nuts.

An excessive intake of folate is a concern because it can mask the symptoms of vitamin B_{12} deficiency. This masking may lead to a delay in treatment until damage from the vitamin B_{12} deficiency becomes permanent.

VITAMIN B_{12}

Vitamin B_{12}, or **cobalamin,** is a B vitamin that is found only in animal products. Foods like beef, chicken, and fish are excellent dietary sources, but plant foods do not provide this vitamin unless they have been contaminated with other sources of vitamin B_{12}, or have been fortified with it.

Vitamin B_{12} is necessary for the maintenance of myelin, which insulates nerves and is necessary for nerve transmission. Vitamin B_{12} is also a coenzyme for a reaction that rearranges carbon atoms so that certain fatty acids can be used to generate energy and for a reaction that synthesizes the amino acid methionine from homocysteine. This conversion of homocysteine to methionine also converts an inactive form of folate to the active coenzyme form that is needed for DNA synthesis. Because of the need for vitamin B_{12} in folate metabolism, a deficiency of vitamin B_{12} can cause a folate deficiency and excesses of folate can mask a vitamin B_{12} deficiency.

Because vitamin B_{12} is needed to activate folate, some of the deficiency symptoms are the same for these two vitamins—elevated blood homocysteine levels and macrocytic anemia. Because vitamin B_{12} is needed to maintain the myelin sheath that coats the nerves, vitamin B_{12} deficiency also causes neurological symptoms including tingling and numbness, abnormalities in gait, memory loss, and disorientation.

Vitamin B_{12} in food is bound to protein. In order to be absorbed, it must be released by protein-digesting enzymes and bound to **intrinsic factor**, a protein that is secreted by the stomach. Only a very small percentage of vitamin B_{12} can be absorbed without intrinsic factor.

Vitamin B_{12} deficiency takes a long time to develop even if the diet is deficient because the vitamin is efficiently recycled. It is secreted into the gastrointestinal tract in bile, and, in a healthy person, most of the vitamin B_{12} is reabsorbed. Deficiencies occur in individuals who consume no animal products and in those who are unable to absorb the vitamin. One cause of vitamin B_{12} **malabsorption** is pernicious anemia. This is a disease in which the body's immune system destroys the cells that produce intrinsic factor. Without intrinsic factor, adequate amounts of dietary vitamin B_{12} cannot be absorbed, and that which is excreted in bile cannot be reabsorbed. **Atrophic gastritis** can also cause vitamin B_{12} deficiency. Atrophic gastritis is an inflammation of the stomach that causes a reduction in stomach acid. It reduces the absorption of vitamin B_{12} that is bound to proteins in food. This condition occurs in 10% to 30% of individuals over 50 years of age. Because it is so common, it is recommended that individuals over the age of 50 meet their RDA for vitamin B_{12} by consuming fortified foods or by taking a vitamin B_{12}-containing supplement. The vitamin B_{12} in fortified foods and supplements is not bound to proteins so it is absorbed even when stomach acid is low. No UL has been established for vitamin B_{12}.

VITAMIN C

Throughout history, the vitamin C deficiency disease **scurvy** has been the downfall of armies, navies, and explorers. The reason vitamin C deficiency was such a problem is that this vitamin is found in fresh fruits and vegetables—foods that spoil quickly and do not transport well on long voyages. In the seventeenth century, Sir Richard Hawkins observed that scurvy could be cured by consuming citrus fruit. Unfortunately, this did not become common practice until about 150 years later when it became mandatory for British sailors to include lime or lemon juice in their rations (earning them the name "limeys").

Vitamin C, also known as **ascorbate** or **ascorbic acid,** is a water-soluble vitamin that is needed for the synthesis and maintenance of **collagen.** Collagen is the most abundant protein in the body and the predominant protein in connective tissue. Without sufficient vitamin C, collagen cannot be synthesized or maintained (Figure 7.2). This causes the symptoms of scurvy, which include poor wound healing, weakened blood vessels, bone fractures, bleeding gums, and loose teeth.

Vitamin C is also needed for the synthesis of some neurotransmitters and hormones, bile acids, and carnitine, which is a substance that is needed to break down fatty acids. Vitamin C also acts as an antioxidant, a substance that protects against damage from reactive oxygen molecules such as free radicals. These reactive molecules damage DNA, proteins, carbohydrates, and unsaturated fatty acids by stealing their electrons. Antioxidants protect the body by destroying reactive oxygen molecules before

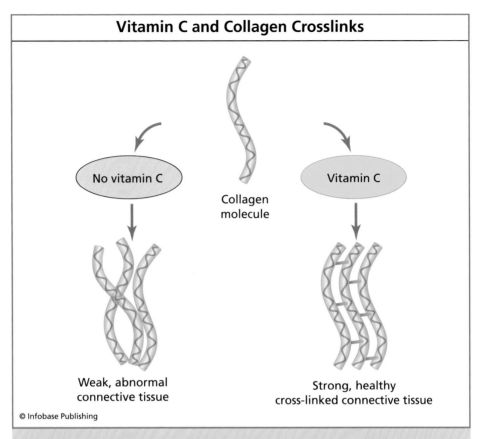

Vitamin C and Collagen Crosslinks

No vitamin C

Collagen molecule

Vitamin C

Weak, abnormal connective tissue

Strong, healthy cross-linked connective tissue

© Infobase Publishing

FIGURE 7.2 Vitamin C is needed to form the bonds that link collagen molecules together, making connective tissue strong. When vitamin C is deficient, the bonds cannot form and the result is connective tissue that is weak and comes apart easily.

they can do damage. Some antioxidants are produced in the body; others, including vitamin C, vitamin E, and the mineral selenium, are dietary constituents. The antioxidant properties of vitamin C also allow it to regenerate the active antioxidant form of vitamin E and enhance iron absorption by keeping iron in its more readily absorbed form.

The best-known source of vitamin C is citrus fruits such as oranges, lemons, and limes. Other good sources include straw-berries, cantaloupe, tomatoes, peppers, potatoes, leafy green vegetables, and vegetables in the cabbage family, such as broccoli, cauliflower, bok choy, and Brussels sprouts.

In the United States today, scurvy is rare, but vitamin C is the most commonly consumed vitamin supplement. One-third of the population of the United States takes supplements of vitamin C in the hope that it will prevent or reduce cold symptoms. Scientific studies have shown that vitamin C does not reduce the incidence of colds but can reduce the duration and severity of cold symptoms. Taking supplements of vitamin C is generally not harmful because it is relatively nontoxic. However, intakes of more than 1 gram can cause diarrhea, nausea, and abdominal cramps. When vitamin C tablets are chewed, its acidic nature can erode tooth enamel.

VITAMIN A

For generations mothers have been telling their children that eating carrots will help them see better in the dark. It turns out that they were right. Carrots are a good source of **beta-carotene (β-carotene)**, which can be turned into vitamin A in your body. Vitamin A is needed for vision; one of the first signs of a deficiency in this vitamin is difficulty seeing in dim light or at night, a condition called night blindness.

Vitamin A is a fat-soluble vitamin that is found in the diet both as **retinoids** and **carotenoids**. Retinoids are preformed vitamin A, while carotenoids, such as β-carotene, are yellow-orange pigments that can be converted to retinoids in the body. Because retinoids and carotenoids are fat soluble, they are absorbed along with dietary fat. In the small intestine, they, along with other fat-soluble food components, combine with bile acids to form micelles, which facilitate their absorption. Retinoids are absorbed more efficiently than carotenoids. Retinoids and carotenoids absorbed from the diet are incorporated into lipoproteins, which transport them, along with dietary fat, from the intestine to body cells. Vitamin A is stored in the liver. To move from liver stores to the tissues, preformed vitamin A must be transported by retinol-binding protein.

Vitamin A Functions

There are three different retinoids in the body: retinal, retinol, and retinoic acid. Retinol is the form of vitamin A that circulates in the blood. It can be converted into retinal, which is important in the visual cycle. In this cycle, which occurs in the retina of the eye, retinal combines with the protein opsin to form the visual pigment **rhodopsin** (Figure 7.3). When light strikes the retina, the retinal in

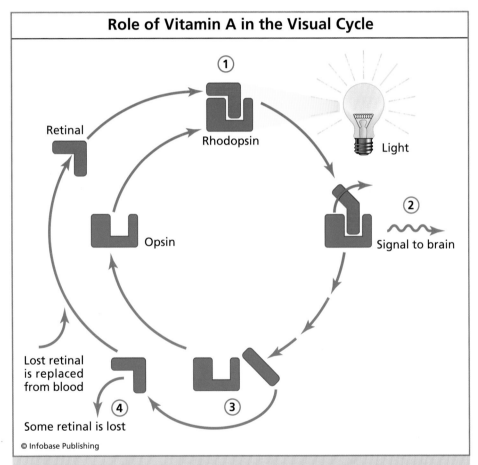

FIGURE 7.3 Vitamin A is an important part of the visual cycle. In the eye, retinal combines with opsin to form rhodopsin (1). When light strikes rhodopsin, retinal changes shape, causing a nerve signal to be sent to the brain (2) and retinal to separate from opsin (3). Some of this retinol is lost and must be replaced from retinoids in the blood (4).

rhodopsin is changed from a curved molecule into a straight one. This change causes retinal to separate from opsin and sends a nerve signal to the brain. After the light stimulus has passed, the retinal can be converted back to its curved form and rhodopsin can be regenerated. Each time this cycle occurs, some retinal is lost and must be replaced by vitamin A from the blood. If vitamin A is deficient, the retinal cannot be replaced and night blindness occurs.

The retinoic acid form of vitamin A can be made from retinol or retinal. It is needed for normal **cell differentiation**, which is the process whereby immature cells change in structure and function to form mature specialized cells. Retinoic acid affects cell differentiation by directing **gene expression**. This means that retinoic acid determines which genes are turned on and which are turned off. In this way, it controls which proteins a cell will produce. For example, vitamin A is needed for the proper differentiation of cells in epithelial tissue—the tissue that lines body cavities and covers surfaces. When vitamin A is present, new epithelial cells differentiate into mucus-secreting cells. When vitamin A is deficient, new epithelial cells do not differentiate correctly and, instead of becoming mucus-secreting cells, they become cells that produce **keratin**, a protein that makes up hair and fingernails. When this occurs, the tissue becomes hard and dry and cracks easily leading to infection. The eye is particularly susceptible to damage when vitamin A is deficient because the mucus secretions are necessary to lubricate the eye, to wash away dirt, and to destroy bacteria. When mucus-secreting cells are replaced by keratin-secreting cells, the surface of the eye becomes dry and cloudy, eventually resulting in sores and infection. **Xerophthalmia** is a spectrum of eye conditions resulting from vitamin A deficiency. If not treated early, it can result in permanent blindness.

Vitamin A is important for the immune system because it is needed for the differentiation of cells into the various types of immune cells. When vitamin A is deficient, immune function is impaired and the risk of illness and infection due to defective epithelial tissue barriers is increased. This further increases the risk of eye infections leading to blindness. Vitamin A is also important for reproduction because of its role in cell differentiation and because it is involved in directing cells to form the shapes and patterns needed for a fully developed organism.

Much of the β-carotene from the diet is converted into retinoids and provides vitamin A function. However, some unconverted carotenoids also reach the blood and tissues, where they may function as antioxidants.

Dietary Sources of Vitamin A

Vitamin A in the diet comes from both animal and plant sources. Retinoids are found in animal foods such as liver, fish, egg yolks, and dairy products. Margarine and nonfat and reduced-fat milk are fortified with retinoids because they are often consumed in place of butter and whole milk, which are good natural sources of this vitamin. Plant foods contain carotenoids. β-carotene is plentiful in yellow-orange fruits and vegetables such as carrots, squash, and apricots, as well as in leafy greens where the yellow-orange pigment is masked by chlorophyll's green color. Other carotenoids that can be converted into vitamin A include **alpha-carotene,** which is found in leafy green vegetables, carrots, and squash; and **beta-cryptoxanthin,** which is found in papaya, red bell peppers, and squash. **Lycopene, lutein,** and **zeaxanthin** are carotenoids that cannot be converted into vitamin A.

Vitamin A Deficiency and Toxicity

Although uncommon in developed countries, vitamin A deficiency is a major public health problem in the developing world, particularly for children. Children who are deficient in vitamin A are anemic, grow poorly, and are at increased risk for infections. It is estimated that 250 million preschool children worldwide are vitamin A deficient and 250,000 to 500,000 go blind annually due to vitamin A deficiency. A very low-fat diet, providing less than 10 grams per day, can cause a vitamin A deficiency because vitamin A cannot be absorbed from the diet without adequate fat. Protein deficiency can also precipitate vitamin A deficiency because retinol binding protein is needed to transport the vitamin from stores in the liver.

Consumption of too much preformed vitamin A can be deadly. Common foods do not contain enough vitamin A to be a problem, but supplements of preformed vitamin A have the potential to deliver a toxic dose. Chronic toxicity occurs when preformed vitamin A doses as low as ten times the RDA are consumed for a period of months to years. Symptoms of chronic toxicity include weight loss, dry and cracked skin, muscle and joint pain, liver damage, and bone abnormalities. Birth defects are also associated with high dietary intakes of preformed vitamin A. Because of their potential to cause birth defects, derivatives of vitamin A that are used to treat acne (such as Retin A and Accutane) should never be used by pregnant women. Carotenoids are not toxic, but a high intake of them can cause your skin to turn orange, a condition called **hypercarotenemia**. To reduce the risk of toxicity, most supplements provide vitamin A as carotenoids.

VITAMIN D

Vitamin D is a fat-soluble vitamin needed for healthy bones. It is known as the sunshine vitamin because it is made in our skin when skin is exposed to sunlight. Vitamin D is only essential in

PASS ON THE POLAR BEAR LIVER

In general, it is not possible to consume a toxic amount of a vitamin from a natural food. An exception is polar bear liver. It contains about 100,000 μg of vitamin A in just one ounce, more than 100 times the RDA. In 1857, Arctic explorers who consumed polar bear liver developed toxicity symptoms that included drowsiness, irritability, headache, and vomiting, with subsequent peeling of the skin. Why is polar bear liver so high in vitamin A? Vitamin A is stored in the liver and polar bears eat fish, seals, and walruses, all of which have enormous amounts of vitamin A stored in their livers.

the diet when exposure to sunlight is limited or when the body's ability to make it is reduced. Lack of sunshine contributed to the high incidence of vitamin D deficiency that took place in Europe during the Industrial Revolution. At this time, people moved from rural villages to big cities to work indoors in factories. Even when they were outside, smog and tall buildings blocked the sunlight, which helped contribute to the deficiency. Today, lack of sun exposure and low dietary intakes continue to put many people at risk of having suboptimal levels of vitamin D.

Vitamin D Functions

Vitamin D is needed for calcium absorption and to maintain the proper ratio of calcium and phosphorus in the blood. Whether it is made in the skin or consumed in the diet, vitamin D must be converted to its active form in order to function. This involves the addition of 2 hydroxyl (OH) groups to its chemical structure. The first OH is added by the liver and the second is added by the kidney. The activation of vitamin D occurs in response to **parathyroid hormone (PTH),** which is released when blood calcium levels drop too low.

Active vitamin D, like vitamin A, acts by affecting gene expression. It functions in a number of locations in the body. In the intestine, it turns on the synthesis of calcium transport proteins, which increase the absorption of calcium from the diet. In the bones, active vitamin D causes cells to differentiate into cells that break down bone. The breakdown of bone releases calcium and phosphorus into the blood. Vitamin D is also now believed to play a role in preventing cells from transforming into cancer cells.

Vitamin D Deficiency and Toxicity

A vitamin D deficiency causes a reduction in calcium absorption. Without sufficient calcium, bones become weak. In children, vitamin D deficiency is called **rickets**. Rickets is characterized by narrow rib cages known as pigeon breasts and legs that bow because they are unable to support the body's weight (Figure 7.4). In adults, vitamin D deficiency is called **osteomalacia**. This condition is characterized by a reduction in the mineral content of bone and can lead to increased bone fractures. Osteomalacia is common in adults who suffer from kidney failure because the activation of vitamin D by the kidney is reduced. Vitamin D deficiency is also now believed to increase the risk of developing and dying from colon, breast, ovarian, and prostate cancer, and it may play a role in the development of a number of other chronic conditions such as type 1 diabetes, multiple sclerosis, and high blood pressure.

The fortification of milk with vitamin D has helped to greatly reduce rickets in most developed countries, but vitamin D deficiency may be increasing due to insufficient sun exposure and low dietary intake. Factors that reduce vitamin D synthesis in the skin include living at high latitudes, having dark skin pigmentation, and covering the skin with clothing or sunscreen. People who live at latitudes greater than 40 degrees north or south, may not receive enough sunlight during the winter months to synthesize adequate amounts of vitamin D. People with dark skin pigmentation have an increased risk of vitamin D deficiency because their dark pigment blocks the ultraviolet light from the sun from penetrating into the deeper layers of the skin where most vitamin D is synthesized; this reduces vitamin D synthesis by as much as 99%. Wearing concealing clothing and applying sunscreen also blocks the ultraviolet light that is needed to produce vitamin D. Older adults are at increased risk of vitamin D deficiency because they generally spend less time in the sun and the ability to synthesize vitamin D in the skin decreases with age. Those with dark skin

(opposite) **FIGURE 7.4** This Bangladeshi boy's deformed legs were caused by rickets, a disease that weakens the bones. Bowed legs, the most common symptom of rickets, occurs when not enough calcium and phosphorus is deposited in the leg bones so they are too weak to support the body's weight and bow as the child learns to walk and put weight on his legs. The disease is caused by a deficiency of vitamin D.

pigmentation and those who live in northern climates may need to rely more on dietary sources of the vitamin. However, vitamin D is not widespread in the food supply. Natural sources include egg yolks, liver, and fatty fish such as salmon.

Foods that are fortified with vitamin D include milk, margarine, and some yogurts, cheeses, and breakfast cereals. Milk is also an important source of dietary calcium. Low milk consumption may contribute to vitamin D deficiency in older adults, vegans, and people with lactose intolerance. The recommended intake for vitamin D is 5 µg per day (200 **International Units [IU]** for young adults, 10 µg per day (400 IU) for adults ages 50 to 70, and 15 µg per day (600 IU) for people who are over 70 years old. However, our expanding understanding of the roles that vitamin D plays in the prevention of cancer and other diseases has led many experts to suggest that all children and adults consume 20 to 25 µg per day (800 to 1000 IU) if they are not getting adequate exposure to sunlight.

Too much vitamin D can cause symptoms that include high blood and urine calcium concentrations, deposits of calcium in the blood vessels and kidneys, and heart damage. However, toxicity is rare because the synthesis of vitamin D in the skin is regulated and unfortified foods do not contain toxic amounts. The UL is 50 µg per day (2,000 IU), but it is now believed that amounts well above this may be safe based on the fact that sun exposure can provide an adult with an amount of vitamin D equivalent to consumption of 250 µg per day (10,000 IU).

VITAMIN E

Vitamin E is a fat-soluble vitamin that was first recognized for its important role in the fertility of laboratory rats. The chemical name for vitamin E is **tocopherol** (which is from the Greek words *tos*, meaning "childbirth," and *phero*, "to bring forth").

Vitamin E functions as an antioxidant that neutralizes reactive oxygen compounds before they damage unsaturated fatty acids in cell membranes. After vitamin E is used to eliminate free radicals, its antioxidant function can be restored by vitamin C. Vitamin E is important in maintaining the membrane integrity of red blood cells, cells in nervous tissue, and cells of the immune system. Vitamin E can also protect cells from damage caused by heavy metals, such as lead and mercury, and toxins, such as carbon tetrachloride, benzene, and a variety of drugs and environmental pollutants.

The antioxidant role of vitamin E suggests that it may help reduce the risk of heart disease, cancer, Alzheimer's disease, macular degeneration, and a variety of other chronic diseases. Particular attention has been paid to its potential benefits in guarding against heart disease. As an antioxidant, vitamin E may prevent the oxidation of LDL cholesterol, which is an early step in the development of atherosclerosis. Consuming a diet high in vitamin E has been associated with lower risk of heart disease. However, clinical studies examining the effect of vitamin E supplements have not found them to lower the risk of heart disease. In some cases, in fact, studies have found that the supplements are associated with an increase in the incidence of heart failure, stroke, and death. Thus, although vitamin E supplements are not recommended to prevent heart disease, a diet high in vitamin E and other antioxidants is recommended.

There are several forms of vitamin E that occur naturally in food, but only **alpha-tocopherol, or α-tocopherol,** can meet vitamin E requirements in humans. Synthetic α-tocopherol, found in dietary supplements and fortified foods, provides only half of the biological activity of natural α-tocopherol. Dietary sources of vitamin E include nuts and peanuts; plant oils such as soybean, corn, and sunflower oils; leafy green vegetables; wheat germ; and fortified breakfast cereals.

Vitamin E deficiency is rare because it is plentiful in the food supply and is stored in many of the body's tissues. A deficiency can cause changes in cell membranes; red blood cells and nerve tissue are particularly susceptible. In premature infants, vitamin E deficiency may cause red blood cells to rupture. In adults, vitamin E deficiency is usually characterized by symptoms associated with nerve degeneration, such as poor muscle coordination, weakness, and impaired vision. Vitamin E is relatively nontoxic, but taking supplements containing more than 1,000 mg per day can interfere with the activity of vitamin K.

VITAMIN K

Without vitamin K, a small scratch could cause you to bleed to death. This is because vitamin K is essential for blood clotting. When it is absent, even a bruise or small scratch could be fatal. Rat poison kills rodents by making them vitamin K deficient. The poison's main ingredient is a compound called **warfarin** that inhibits vitamin K activity. When the rats eat it, their blood fails to clot and they bleed to death.

Bacteria that live in our intestines produce some of the vitamin K we need, but some of it must also come from the diet. The best sources are leafy green vegetables such as spinach, broccoli, brussels sprouts, kale, and turnip greens. Vegetable oils including soybean, cottonseed, canola, and olive oil also provide vitamin K. Meats, milk, and eggs provide little of this vitamin.

The major symptom of vitamin K deficiency is abnormal blood clotting. In addition to its role in coagulation, vitamin K is also needed for the synthesis of several proteins involved in bone formation and breakdown. With a vitamin K deficiency, bone mineral density is reduced, and the risk of fractures increases. Deficiency is very rare in the healthy adult population, but it may result from fat malabsorption (because vitamin K is absorbed with fat) or the long-term use of antibiotics, which kill the bacteria in the gastrointestinal tract that are a source of the vitamin. Vitamin K deficiency is a problem in newborns because little of it is transferred to the baby from the mother before birth, breast milk is a poor source, and newborns have no bacteria in their gut to synthesize the vitamin. To ensure normal blood clotting, infants are typically given a vitamin K injection within six hours of birth.

The inability to form blood clots can cause death from excess blood loss, but blood that clots too easily can contribute to heart attacks and strokes. To prevent this, blood thinning medications,

COWS, CLOVER, AND COAGULATION

When President Dwight Eisenhower had a heart attack in 1955, his recovery was aided by an **anticoagulant** drug called sodium warfarin. Warfarin prevents blood from clotting by interfering with the action of vitamin K. It is still used today (under the brand name Coumadin) to prevent fatal blood clots in millions of people. The discovery of warfarin had its beginnings in the 1930s when cows across the Midwestern prairies were bleeding to death from what was called hemorrhagic sweet clover disease. The wheels of science were set in motion on a snowy night in 1933 when a farmer delivered a bale of moldy clover hay, a pail of unclotted blood, and a dead cow to the laboratory of Dr. Carl Link at the University of Wisconsin. Link and his colleagues isolated an anticoagulant substance called dicoumarol from the moldy clover. They found that the dicoumarol was formed by the action of mold on a compound normally present in the clover. As a result, when the cows consumed the moldy clover, they ate the dicoumarol and their blood failed to clot. Dicoumarol was the first anticoagulant that could be taken orally rather than by injection. Warfarin is a more potent derivative of dicoumarol.

such as coumadin, are routinely prescribed to heart patients. Individuals taking these medications may need to avoid supplements that contain vitamin K because they may reduce the effectiveness of the medication.

REVIEW

Vitamins are small organic compounds that are essential in the diet in small amounts to promote and regulate body functions. The water-soluble vitamins include the B vitamins and vitamin C. Thiamin, riboflavin, niacin, biotin, and pantothenic acid are needed as coenzymes in the reactions that provide energy from carbohydrates, fat, and protein. Vitamin B_6 is particularly important for amino acid metabolism. Folate is necessary for DNA synthesis and thus is essential for cell division; adequate intake of the folic acid form of folate before and during pregnancy may prevent birth defects called neural tube defects. Vitamin B_{12} is essential for nerve health and for the metabolism of homocysteine, folate, and fatty acids. Vitamin C is essential for the health of connective tissue and acts as an antioxidant. The fat-soluble vitamins include vitamins A, D, E, and K. Vitamin A is needed for vision and for the growth and differentiation of cells. Some carotenoids such as β-carotene can be converted into vitamin A. Vitamin D promotes calcium absorption, so it is important for bone health. It can be made in the skin by exposure to sunlight, so if sun exposure is sufficient, it is not needed in the diet. Vitamin E is a fat-soluble antioxidant that protects cell membranes from oxidative damage. Vitamin K is needed for blood clotting.

8

MINERALS

inerals—aren't those rocks? Of course, but many of the same minerals found in rocks are also found in the human body. The calcium in a limestone cliff, the salt in sea water, and the iron in your skillet are the same as the calcium in your bones, the salt in your tears, and the iron in your blood. To stay healthy, humans need to consume these substances in their diets.

WHAT ARE MINERALS?

Minerals are **inorganic** elements that the body needs to provide structure and regulate the functions of the body. Some minerals are an integral part of bone structure; some play very specific roles in transporting oxygen and regulating blood glucose levels. Many minerals serve as **cofactors**, which are ions or other molecules that are required for enzyme activity.

The **major minerals** include sodium, potassium, chloride, calcium, phosphorus, magnesium, and sulfur; they are called

139

major because either we need a lot of them, more than 100 mg
in the daily diet, or because they are present in the body in
amounts greater than 0.01% of body weight. The **trace elements**
are minerals required by the body in an amount of 100 mg or
less per day, or are present in the body in an amount of 0.01% or
less of body weight. They include iron, zinc, copper, manganese,
selenium, iodine, chromium, fluoride, and molybdenum. There
are also other trace elements found in the body but for many of
these, it has not been determined whether or not they are dietary
essentials.

Minerals are found in foods from both plant and animal
sources. For some minerals, the amount present in foods is pre-
dictable because the minerals are regulated components of the
plant or animal. For instance, iron is a component of muscle tissue; therefore, it is found in consistent amounts in meat. For other
minerals, the amounts present may vary depending on conditions
where the food is produced. For instance, the selenium content
of plants depends on the selenium concentration in the soil and
water where the plant is grown. Food processing and refining
also affect the mineral content of foods. Iron, selenium, zinc, and
copper are lost when wheat is refined to make white flour; iron is
added when white flour is enriched.

HOW MUCH DO YOU NEED?

The amount of each mineral that needs to be consumed to prevent deficiency and promote health depends on the person's age,
gender, and life stage. Recommendations for mineral intake have
been made by the DRIs (Table 8.1). These recommendations must
take into account the mineral's **bioavailability**. Bioavailability is a
measure of how much of the mineral is available to the body after
the food is eaten. It may be increased or decreased by constituents
of the diet and conditions in the body. For example, iron is better
absorbed when it is consumed with orange juice; calcium is better
absorbed during pregnancy.

Components of the diet that can reduce mineral bioavailability include fiber, **phytates, oxalates,** and **tannins**. Fiber is found in grains, fruits, and vegetables; phytates are found in whole grains; oxalates are found in greens and chocolate; and tannins are found in tea and some grains. Foods that are high in these substances can reduce mineral absorption. For example, much of the iron in spinach is unavailable because it is bound to oxalates. There are

TABLE 8.1 RECOMMENDED MINERAL INTAKES

Mineral	Recommended Intake Per Day for Adults	Tolerable Upper Intake Level (UL)
Sodium	1,500–2,300 mg	2,300 mg
Potassium	At least 4,700 mg	Not determined
Chloride	2,300–3,600 mg	3,600 mg
Calcium	1,000–1,200 mg	2,500 mg
Phosphorus	700 mg	Not determined
Magnesium	310–420 mg	350 mg from supplements
Sulfur	None specified	Not determined
Iron	8–18 mg	45 mg
Zinc	8–11 mg	Not determined
Copper	900 µg	10,000 µg
Manganese	1.8–2.3 mg	11 mg
Selenium	55 µg	400 µg
Iodine	150 µg	1,100 µg
Chromium	25–35 µg	Not determined
Fluoride	3–4 mg	10 mg
Molybdenum	45 µg	2000 µg

also substances in the diet that promote mineral absorption. For example, including vitamin C in a meal that contains iron can enhance the absorption of iron sixfold. Minerals also interact with each other. A high intake of zinc, for example, can reduce copper absorption. All of these interactions tend to balance out in a varied diet and usually do not affect mineral status. However, large doses of mineral supplements may upset the balance, leading to a deficiency or toxicity.

THE ELECTROLYTES: SODIUM, POTASSIUM, AND CHLORIDE

Electrolytes are negatively and positively charged ions that conduct electricity when dissolved in water. Chemically speaking, many minerals are electrolytes, but when discussing nutrition, the term electrolyte is generally used to refer to sodium, potassium, and chloride, the principal electrolytes that are found in body fluids.

What Do Electrolytes Do?

Sodium, potassium, and chloride help regulate the amount of water in the body and the distribution of water between different areas or compartments of the body. For example, when the concentration of sodium in the blood increases, water moves into the blood by osmosis, causing an increase in blood volume and blood pressure. The electrolytes are also important for nerve conduction and muscle contraction. Sodium is the most abundant positively charged electrolyte outside the body's cells and potassium is the principal positively charged ion inside the body's cells. The cell membrane inhibits the flow of sodium into the cell and the flow of potassium out of the cell, but small amounts do leak across. At the nerve cell membrane, more potassium leaks out of the cell than sodium leaks in, causing the number of positively charged ions just outside the membrane to be greater than the number of them inside the membrane. This difference in the electrical charge inside and outside the membrane is called the membrane potential. When a nerve is stimulated, it causes the membrane to allow sodium to rush into the cell. This causes a change in the membrane potential that travels along the nerve and is known as a nerve impulse. A similar mechanism causes stimulation of the muscle cell membrane and leads to muscle contraction.

Electrolytes in Our Diet

The modern diet is typically low in potassium and high in sodium. A typical American diet contains about 9 grams of salt; salt is 40% sodium and 60% chloride, so this is equivalent to 3.6 grams of sodium and 5.4 grams of chloride. These amounts are well above the recommended upper intake levels of 2.3 and 3.6

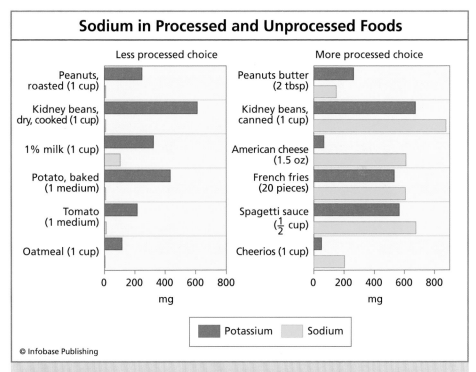

FIGURE 8.1 Many Americans eat processed, packaged foods that are high in sodium. Eating unprocessed foods, such as fresh fruits and vegetables, can reduce the sodium and increase the potassium intakes to meet recommended dietary guidelines.

grams per day, respectively. Most of the salt in the American diet comes from processed foods (Figure 8.1). In contrast, we eat less than the recommended amount of potassium. Most of the potassium in our diet comes from unprocessed foods such as fruits, vegetables, whole grains, and fresh meats.

Balancing Electrolytes In and Out

The intake of sodium varies greatly among different populations. For example, in northern China, sodium chloride intake is greater than 13.9 grams per day, while in the Kalahari Desert, it is less than 1.7 grams per day. Nonetheless, blood levels of sodium are not significantly different among these groups. This is because levels of electrolytes are closely regulated.

Sodium and chloride levels in the body are regulated by the intake of both water and salt. When salt intake is high, thirst is stimulated to increase water intake. When salt intake is very low, an appetite for salt stimulates the individual to increase salt intake. These mechanisms help ensure that appropriate proportions of salt and water are consumed. The kidneys, however, are the primary regulator of sodium, chloride, and potassium balance in the body. Excretion of sodium in the urine is decreased when intake is low and increased when intake is high. Because water follows sodium by osmosis, the ability of the kidneys to conserve sodium provides a mechanism to conserve body water.

Changes in the amount of sodium in the blood affect blood pressure, and changes in blood pressure trigger the production and release of proteins and hormones that alter the amount of sodium, and hence water, that is retained by the kidneys. A decrease in blood pressure leads to the release of the hormone aldosterone, which acts on the kidneys to increase sodium and chloride reabsorption. Water follows the reabsorbed sodium, resulting in an increase in blood volume and, consequently, blood pressure.

As with sodium and chloride, the kidneys regulate potassium excretion to maintain a relatively constant amount of potassium in the body. If blood levels begin to rise, mechanisms are activated to stimulate the cellular uptake of potassium. This short-term regulation prevents the amount of potassium in the extracellular fluid from reaching lethally high levels. The long-term regulation of potassium balance depends on aldosterone release, which causes the kidney to excrete potassium and retain sodium.

Electrolyte deficiencies are rare in healthy individuals, but they may occur as a result of losses from vomiting, diarrhea, increased urinary losses, and excessive sweating. Symptoms of deficiency include poor appetite, nausea, muscle cramps, confusion, apathy, constipation, and irregular heartbeat. Electrolyte toxicity is also rare, but it does occur when supplements are consumed in excess or when kidney function is compromised.

Electrolytes and Blood Pressure

Blood pressure is the pressure that the blood exerts against blood vessel walls. Normal blood pressure is less than 120/80 millimeters of mercury. Blood pressure increases when blood volume is too high or the blood vessels become narrow and inelastic. High blood pressure, known as hypertension, is defined as a blood pressure measurement that is consistently 140/90 mm of mercury or greater. Hypertension increases the risk of atherosclerosis, heart attack, stroke, and kidney disease.

The risk of developing hypertension is increased by a family history of hypertension, excess body weight, lack of exercise, and certain dietary patterns. Diets high in salt are associated with a higher incidence of hypertension, whereas diets high in potassium, calcium, magnesium, and fiber, are associated with a lower incidence of hypertension. The recommendation that sodium intake should be kept below 1.5 g per day is based on the fact that a high intake of sodium may cause an increase in blood pressure. Because there are many dietary factors involved in blood pressure regulation, the **DASH diet (Dietary Approaches to Stop Hypertension)**, is recommended to keep blood pressure in the normal range. This dietary pattern is high in fruits, vegetables, low-fat dairy products, whole grains, and lean meats, making it high in potassium, calcium, magnesium, and fiber, and moderate in salt and fat.

CALCIUM

"Drink your milk." Children hear this command from their mothers while adults hear it from their doctors. This is because milk is an excellent source of calcium. Calcium is needed for the development and maintenance of strong healthy bones. If calcium intake is low in childhood, the bones may not achieve their maximum strength. If intake is low in adulthood, bone strength may be lost more quickly than is normal. In either case, the result may be an increase in bone fractures later in life.

Calcium Functions

Calcium is the most abundant mineral in the body. It is important for the maintenance of bones and teeth where it is part of a solid crystalline material called hydroxyapatite. Calcium also plays extremely important roles in cell communication and the regulation of body processes. It is needed to release neurotransmitters so that a nerve signal can pass from a nerve to the target cell. Inside the muscle cells, the presence of calcium allows the two muscle proteins, actin and myosin, to interact to cause muscle contraction. Calcium also plays a role in blood pressure regulation and blood clotting.

Getting Calcium Into Your Body

Most of the calcium in the American diet comes from dairy products such as milk, cheese, and yogurt. Other good sources include tofu, legumes, leafy green vegetables, and fish that are consumed with the bones, such as sardines. Foods fortified with calcium such as breakfast cereals and juices also make an important contribution to the calcium content of the American diet. Individuals who do not meet their calcium needs with diet alone can benefit from calcium supplementation.

Adequate vitamin D is important for calcium absorption. Although some calcium can be absorbed in the absence of vitamin D, vitamin D-dependent absorption accounts for most of the calcium absorbed when intakes are low to moderate. Other dietary factors also affect calcium absorption. Calcium absorption is increased by the presence of the sugar lactose but is reduced by the presence of fiber, phytates from whole grains, and oxalates from foods such as spinach, sweet potatoes, and rhubarb. Chocolate also contains oxalates, but chocolate milk is still a good source of calcium. Calcium absorption also varies with the body's life stage; it is increased when the need for calcium is high, such as during infancy and pregnancy.

Excessive calcium consumption occurs primarily from the use of supplements. Too much calcium may cause kidney stones in susceptible individuals, and may interfere with the absorption of other minerals.

Regulating Blood Calcium

Maintaining calcium homeostasis is critical to nerve transmission and muscle contraction, and hence to the body's survival. Even small changes in blood calcium levels trigger regulatory mechanisms that restore them to normal levels. The hormones parathyroid hormone (PTH), which raises blood calcium, and **calcitonin,** which lowers blood calcium, are essential to calcium regulation.

When blood calcium levels drop, PTH is released from the parathyroid gland and acts in three different ways to raise blood calcium levels. First, at the bone, it stimulates bone breakdown to release calcium into the blood; second, at the kidney, it reduces calcium excretion so more calcium is retained in the blood; and third, it signals the activation of vitamin D by the kidney. Active vitamin D then enhances the absorption of dietary calcium from the intestine (Figure 8.2). When blood calcium levels rise above the normal range, the release of PTH is stopped and the hormone calcitonin is released from the thyroid gland. Calcitonin acts on the bone to inhibit the release of calcium, allowing blood calcium levels to decrease to normal.

Calcium and Bone Health

The ability to maintain blood calcium levels by removing calcium from bone prevents life-threatening drops in blood calcium and is therefore beneficial over the short term. However, if calcium

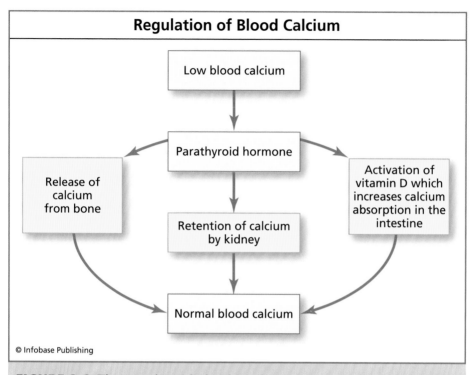

FIGURE 8.2 The parathyroid gland produces a hormone that regulates the calcium levels in the blood. When calcium levels are low, parathyroid hormone acts at the bone to release calcium into the bloodstream and the kidneys to inhibit calcium excretion and activate vitamin D.

removal continues over the long term, it results in weakened bones that are susceptible to fractures. This condition is known as **osteoporosis**. Osteoporosis is a public health concern in the United States, where about 44 million people aged 50 or older have osteoporosis or are at risk for it due to low bone mass. Osteoporosis is estimated to cause 1.5 million fractures annually.

Bone is an active living tissue that is constantly being broken down and reformed. In growing children and adolescents, bone formation occurs more rapidly than bone breakdown, which allows the bones to grow in size and density. Bone deposition continues to outpace bone breakdown into young adulthood when maximal bone density or peak bone mass is achieved. After about age 35 to 40, bone breakdown exceeds formation, so bone is slowly lost and bone density declines. If the **peak bone mass** achieved in young adulthood is high enough, bones will remain strong into old age, despite the normal loss of bone that occurs later in life.

The risk of developing osteoporosis depends on how dense the bones are and the rate at which bone is lost. The risk increases with age because bone is lost continuously after about age 45. Osteoporosis is more common in thin, light-weight people because they have lower bone mass than bigger, heavier people. It is more common in women than men because men have denser bones and because women lose bone faster than men, due to an acceleration in bone loss after menopause. African Americans have a lower risk of osteoporosis than Caucasians or Southeast Asians because they have denser bones. Smoking and alcohol use increase the risk of osteoporosis and weight-bearing exercise such as walking and jogging increase bone density and reduce risk.

A number of dietary factors affect the risk of osteoporosis. A diet that is adequate in calcium and vitamin D helps ensure a high peak bone mass early in life and reduces bone loss later in life. Adequate dietary protein is necessary for bone health, and higher intakes of zinc, magnesium, potassium, fiber, and vita-min C—nutrients that are plentiful in fruits and vegetables—are associated with greater bone mass. The risk of osteoporosis is increased by diets that are low in calcium and vitamin D and by high intakes of phytates, oxalates, and tannins, which interfere with calcium absorption. High dietary sodium may increase risk because it increases calcium loss in the urine. The risk of osteo-porosis can be minimized by a lifelong diet rich in fruits and vegetables, adequate in calcium and vitamin D, and not excessive in phosphorus, protein, or sodium. Once osteoporosis has devel-oped, there are medications that can help restore lost bone, but it is far better to get plenty of exercise and consume a diet that helps prevent osteoporosis in the first place.

YOUNG GIRLS WITH OLD BONES

We normally think of osteoporosis as a disease that affects old people, but young female athletes can also be at risk. Female athletes often keep their weight down by limiting what they eat. A low calorie diet combined with a high level of physical activity reduces body fat and can delay the onset of the menstrual cycle or cause it to stop, a condition called *amenorrhea*. Amenorrhea is accompanied by low levels of estrogen, a hormone that is important for bone health. Low estrogen levels decrease calcium absorption from the diet and affect calcium balance at the bone, causing reductions in bone mass and bone-mineral density and an increased risk of bone fractures. The combination of low estrogen levels and poor calcium intake leads to premature bone loss and failure to reach a healthy peak bone mass. These young girls have a condition called the female athlete triad: disordered eating, amenorrhea, and osteoporosis. They have bones more like their grandmothers than like a typical teenage girl. If these girls resume regular menstrual periods by decreasing their training or increasing their calorie intake, they can regain some bone density, but the bones do not completely return to normal density. Reduced bone density puts these athletes at risk of stress fractures as well as more serious fractures of the hip or spine.

PHOSPHORUS

Phosphorus is an important structural component of bones where, along with calcium, it forms hydroxyapatite crystals. Phosphorus also has other structural and regulatory roles. It is a component of phospholipids, which form the basic structure of cell membranes. It is a major constituent of DNA and RNA and is important in energy metabolism because the high-energy bonds of ATP are formed between phosphate groups. Phosphorus, as phosphate, also acts as a **buffer** to regulate the level of acidity in cells.

Phosphorus is found in a wide range of foods. These include dairy products, meats, fish, cereals, eggs, and nuts. Food additives used in baked goods, cheeses, processed meats, and soft drinks also provide phosphorus. Unlike calcium, vitamin D does not need to be available to absorb adequate amounts of phosphorus from the diet.

To support bone mineralization, blood levels of phosphorus must be balanced with calcium levels. This balance is maintained through the actions of vitamin D and parathyroid hormone (PTH) on bone breakdown, absorption of calcium and phosphorus from the intestine, and excretion of calcium and phosphorus by the kidney.

Phosphorus deficiency can affect bone health, but it is rare because this mineral is so widely distributed in foods. The increased use of phosphorus-containing food additives has created concern about excessive phosphorus intake, which can cause bone breakdown. These higher levels of phosphorus are not believed to affect bone health as long as the intake of calcium is adequate.

MAGNESIUM

Magnesium is a component of the green plant pigment chlorophyll, so leafy green vegetables are a good dietary source. Whole grains, nuts, and seeds are also good sources. About half of the magnesium in the diet is absorbed. Absorption is enhanced by the active form of vitamin D and decreased by the presence of phytates and calcium.

Magnesium has many diverse roles throughout the body. It is less plentiful in bone than calcium and phosphorus but is still essential for the maintenance of bone structure. It is involved in regulating calcium homeostasis and is needed for the action of vitamin D and several hormones. It is also a cofactor for many of the enzymes that are involved in providing energy from carbohydrates, fat, and protein. It is essential for maintenance of membrane potentials and proper functioning of the nerves and muscles, including those in the heart. It is important for the synthesis of protein, DNA, and RNA and is needed to stabilize ATP structure. Magnesium may also be involved in blood pressure regulation.

The kidneys regulate blood levels of magnesium so homeostasis can be maintained over a wide range of dietary intakes. Magnesium deficiency is rare, but it may occur in individuals who suffer from alcoholism, malnutrition, and kidney or intestinal disease. The symptoms of magnesium deficiency include nausea, muscle weakness and cramping, irritability, mental derangement, and changes in blood pressure and heartbeat. Toxic effects have not been observed from ingestion of magnesium in foods, but toxicity may occur from concentrated sources such as drugs and supplements that contain magnesium. Toxicity is characterized by nausea, vomiting, low blood pressure, and other cardiovascular changes.

SULFUR

Sulfur is a component of many essential substances in the body. The B vitamins thiamin and biotin contain sulfur in their structure. Sulfur is also part of the structure of glutathione, which is important in detoxifying drugs and protecting cells from oxidative damage. Methionine and cysteine are sulfur-containing amino acids. Sulfur-containing ions are a part of an important buffer system that regulates acid-base balance. Sulfur in the diet comes from the sulfur-containing amino acids in proteins, some sulfur-containing vitamins, and inorganic sulfur compounds used as food preservatives. There is no recommended intake for sulfur, and no deficiencies are known so long as protein needs are met.

IRON

Someone who is tired, irritable, and having trouble concentrating may only need a good night's sleep; or he or she may be suffering from iron deficiency, the most common nutritional deficiency in this country and around the world.

What Does Iron Do?

Iron is needed to deliver oxygen to body cells. Most of the iron in the body is part of hemoglobin, the protein that gives red blood cells their red color. Hemoglobin transports oxygen to and carries carbon dioxide away from the cells for elimination by the lungs. Iron is also a component of the muscle protein **myoglobin,** which stores oxygen for use in the muscle. Iron is part of several proteins needed for the production of ATP. Catalase is an iron-containing enzyme that protects cells from oxidative damage. In addition, several iron-containing proteins are important for drug metabolism and the immune system.

Iron in Our Diet

Iron can be obtained from both animal and plant sources. Much of the iron in animal products is part of a chemical complex called heme. **Heme iron** is plentiful in meat, poultry, and fish and is absorbed more than twice as efficiently as **non-heme iron.** Plant sources of iron, such as leafy green vegetables, legumes, and whole and enriched grains contain only non-heme iron. Non-heme iron also leaches into food from iron cooking utensils such as iron skillets.

Heme iron absorption is not affected by other components of the diet but the proportion of non-heme iron that is absorbed varies depending on the foods consumed with the iron. It is better absorbed if it is consumed in the same meal as beef, fish, or poultry. Consuming non-heme iron with vitamin C can increase absorption six fold. Vitamin C enhances absorption because it is an acid and because it forms a chemical complex with iron that improves its absorption. Fiber, phytates, tannins, and oxalates reduce absorption. The presence of other minerals may also decrease iron absorption.

Regulating Body Iron Levels

Iron is not easily eliminated from the body. Even when red blood cells die, the iron in their hemoglobin is not lost, but recycled to make new red blood cells. Therefore, the amount of iron in the body is controlled by regulating how much is transported from the cells of the intestine to the rest of the body. When body iron is in short supply, the iron transport protein **transferrin** is able to pick up iron from the intestines and deliver it to body cells. When iron is plentiful in the body, more of the iron storage protein **ferritin** is made. This increases the amount of iron that is bound to ferritin in the intestinal cells and reduces the amount of iron picked up by transferrin and transported to other body cells. Iron that is bound to ferritin in the intestinal cells is excreted in the feces when these cells die. Some of the iron that is transported from the intestine is stored in the liver bound to ferritin. When ferritin concentrations in the liver become high, some is converted to an insoluble iron storage protein called hemosiderin.

Iron Deficiency Anemia

In the United States, iron deficiency affects 3% of adolescent girls and women of childbearing age and 2% of children aged one to two years. When iron is deficient, sufficient hemoglobin cannot be made and the red blood cells that are formed are small, pale, and unable to deliver adequate oxygen to the tissues (Figure 8.3). This condition is known as **iron deficiency anemia**. Symptoms of iron deficiency anemia include fatigue, weakness, headache, decreased work capacity, an inability to maintain body temperature in a cold environment, changes in behavior, decreased resistance to infection, impaired development in infants, and an increased risk of lead poisoning in young children.

Groups at risk of iron deficiency include women of reproductive age, pregnant women, infants, adolescents, and athletes. Women of reproductive age are at risk for iron deficiency anemia because of iron loss due to menstruation. Pregnant women are at risk because iron needs increase to expand maternal blood volume and allow the growth of other maternal tissues and the fetus. Infants and adolescents are at risk for this deficiency because their rapid growth increases the need for iron. Athletes are susceptible to iron deficiency because prolonged training increases losses and some athletes do not consume enough in their diets.

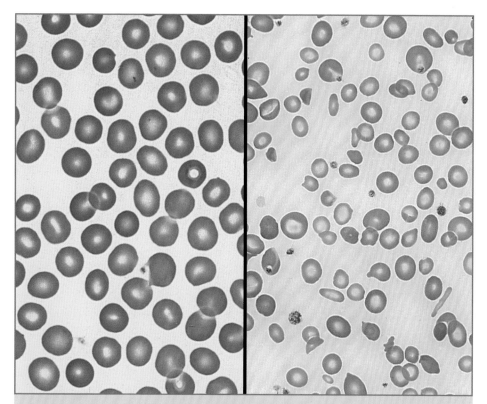

FIGURE 8.3 Iron deficiency anemia prevents the body from producing enough hemoglobin, the component of blood that transports oxygen throughout the body. Healthy red blood cells (*left*) are rich in hemoglobin, while anemic red blood cells are small and pale (*right*).

Too Much Iron Can Be Deadly

Even though iron is essential for health, it can also be deadly. Ingestion of a single large dose damages the intestinal lining, alters body acidity, and can cause shock and liver failure. Iron supplement overdose is the most common form of poisoning in children less than six years of age. Too much body iron, or iron overload, can occur in individuals who require frequent transfusions but the most common cause is **hemochromatosis**. This is a genetic condition that allows increased iron absorption. The accumulation of excess iron that occurs in hemochromatosis darkens

> ## BLOODLETTING
>
> Bloodletting is the withdrawal of blood from a patient for the purpose of curing or preventing an illness or disease. For almost 2,000 years, from ancient times up to the late nineteenth century, it was the most commonly performed medical procedure. It was used to treat a wide variety of aliments and sometimes so much blood was removed that the patient fainted. Today, we know that bloodletting causes more harm than good for most conditions, but a modern version of the procedure is used to treat hemochromatosis. Removing blood also removes iron and prevents the complications of iron overload. Rather than being called "bloodletting" the procedure is now called "therapeutic phlebotomy." Unfortunately, many people with hemochromatosis don't take advantage of this simple treatment because they don't know they have inherited this condition until organ damage has already occurred. Hemochromatosis is the most common inherited disease in Caucasian populations in North America, Australia, and Europe. In the United States, it affects about 1 in 200 to 1 in 500 individuals. To be effective, the bloodletting must begin before the organs are damaged, so early identification of people with this disease through genetic screening is essential in preventing complications.

the skin and causes heart and liver damage, diabetes, and certain types of cancer.

COPPER

It is logical that too little iron in the diet can cause iron deficiency anemia, but surprisingly, too little copper can also cause iron deficiency anemia. Copper is a component of a copper-containing protein that is needed to convert iron into a form that can bind to transferrin for transport from the intestinal cells. Even if iron intake is adequate, if there is not enough copper, iron cannot be transported to tissues where it is needed and so an iron deficiency occurs. Copper is also needed for the function of a number of proteins and enzymes that are involved in lipid metabolism, connective tissue synthesis, maintenance of heart muscle, and function of the immune and central nervous systems. It is needed for the synthesis of the neurotransmitters norepinephrine and dopamine, the pigment melanin, and several blood clotting factors; copper also protects cells from oxidative damage.

Dietary sources of copper include organ meats, seafood, nuts and seeds, whole grains, and chocolate. Only about 30% to 40% of the copper in a typical diet is absorbed. Copper absorption is enhanced by amino acids and reduced by high intakes of zinc, iron, manganese, molybdenum, and vitamin C.

Copper deficiency is relatively rare and not a problem in North America where the amount of copper in the diet is slightly above the RDA. Copper deficiency has been documented in premature infants and in patients who are fed intravenous solutions that lack copper. In addition to iron deficiency anemia, copper deficiency may cause skeletal abnormalities, impaired growth, degeneration of the heart muscle, degeneration of the nervous system, and changes in hair color and structure. Because of its role in the development and maintenance of the immune system, a diet low in copper decreases the immune response and increases the incidence of infection. Copper toxicity from dietary sources is rare.

ZINC

Zinc may come last in an alphabetical list, but it is the second most common trace element in the body after iron. Zinc is involved in the functioning of nearly 100 different enzymes. These enzymes help protect cells from free radical damage and are needed for the synthesis of DNA and RNA, carbohydrate metabolism, acid-base balance, and folate absorption. Zinc plays a role in the storage and release of insulin, the mobilization of vitamin A from the liver, and the stabilization of cell membranes. Zinc is important in gene expression and therefore is needed for the growth and repair of tissues, the activity of the immune system, and the development of sex organs and bone. Zinc-containing proteins are needed for the activity of vitamin A, vitamin D, and a number of hormones including thyroid hormones, estrogen, and testosterone. Without zinc, these nutrients and hormones cannot bind to DNA to increase or decrease gene expression and, hence, the synthesis of certain proteins.

In the diet, zinc is found in red meat, liver, eggs, dairy products, vegetables, and some seafood. Whole grains are a good source, but refined grains are not because the zinc in these grains is lost in milling and not added back in enrichment. Zinc is better absorbed when it is ingested from animal products than it is from plant sources because the zinc in plants is often bound to phytates, fiber, oxalates, and tannins. Grain products leavened with yeast provide more zinc than unleavened products because the yeast leavening reduces the phytate content.

Severe zinc deficiency is rare in North America, but it is a problem in developing countries. Deficiencies have been reported in populations that consume diets based on cereal proteins from which zinc is poorly absorbed. Symptoms include poor growth and development, skin rashes, impaired reproduction, and decreased immune function. Moderate zinc deficiency is more of a concern in the United States. It can cause a decrease in the number and function of immune cells in the blood and therefore can lead to an increased incidence of infections.

High intakes of zinc can also impair immune function, as well as increase the risk of heart disease and interfere with copper absorption. Zinc is often marketed as a supplement to improve immune function, enhance fertility and sexual performance, and cure the common cold. Supplements have been shown to reduce the incidence of diarrhea and infections in people who have low zinc levels, but there is no evidence that extra zinc is beneficial. Over-supplementation may result in toxicity.

MANGANESE

Only about 10 to 20 milligrams of manganese is present in the body, but it is a key component of some enzymes and an activator of others. Manganese-requiring enzymes are involved in amino acid, carbohydrate, and cholesterol metabolism; cartilage formation; urea synthesis; and the protection of cells from oxidative damage.

The best dietary sources of manganese are whole grains, legumes, nuts, and tea. Manganese absorption increases when intake is low and decreases when intake is high. It is eliminated from the body by excretion into the intestinal tract in bile.

A naturally occurring manganese deficiency has never been reported in humans. Toxicity causes nerve damage but has been reported due to industrial exposure, rather than dietary intake.

SELENIUM

In the early 1930s, selenium was identified as the toxic agent that caused lameness and death in livestock that ate certain plants. About 25 years later, this trace element was recognized as an essential nutrient in humans and other animals. Selenium is important in the body's antioxidant defenses. It is an essential part of the enzyme glutathione peroxidase, which helps neutralize compounds called peroxides so they no longer form free radicals and cause oxidative damage. By reducing free radical formation, selenium can spare some of the need for the antioxidant vitamin E. Selenium is also needed for the synthesis of the thyroid hormones, which regulate the body's metabolic rate.

Dietary sources of selenium include seafood, kidney, liver, and eggs. Grains can be a good source of selenium, depending on the selenium content of the soil where they are grown. Because the amount of selenium in a plant depends on the amount in the soil, soil selenium content can have a significant impact on the selenium intake of populations that consume primarily locally grown food.

Selenium deficiency causes muscle discomfort and weakness. It is uncommon but has been identified in individuals receiving intravenous solutions lacking selenium and in regions of China where the soil is deficient in this mineral and the people consume only locally grown food. In China, selenium deficiency is associated with a form of heart disease called Keshan disease. Keshan disease is believed to be caused by a combination of selenium deficiency and a viral infection. Selenium supplements relieve most of the symptoms of Keshan disease and reduce its incidence. Low intakes of selenium are also associated with an increased incidence of certain types of cancer.

Dietary toxicity occurs in regions of China with very high levels of selenium in the soil and has been reported in the United States because of an error in the manufacture of a supplement. Symptoms include brittle hair and nails, hair and nail loss, and gastrointestinal upset.

IODINE

Iodized salt is salt that has been fortified with iodine. In the United States and Canada fortification of salt with iodine began in the 1920s because iodine deficiency was a serious public health problem around the Great Lakes. The most obvious outward sign of iodine deficiency is an enlarged thyroid gland called a **goiter** (Figure 8.4). A goiter forms because of a lack of iodine, which is needed for the production of thyroid hormones. These hormones regulate basal metabolic rate, growth and development, and promote protein synthesis. When thyroid hormone levels drop, it triggers the release of thyroid-stimulating hormone. This hormone signals the thyroid gland to make more thyroid hormones. If iodine is available, the gland responds and thyroid hormone levels return to normal. If iodine is deficient, the thyroid hormones cannot be made, and thyroid-stimulating hormone continues to signal the thyroid gland. This continuous stimulation causes the thyroid gland to enlarge.

Iodine is found in seawater, so natural dietary sources of iodine include fish, seafood, seaweed, and plants grown close to the sea where the iodine content of the soil is high. Iodine-containing food additives and food contaminants also contribute to the iodine content of the American diet. However, most of the iodine in the American diet comes from iodized salt. Sea salt is not a good source of iodine, because the iodine is lost in the drying process.

Iodine deficiency can occur due to a low iodine intake or the consumption of a diet that is high in goitrogens, which are substances in turnips, rutabaga, cabbage, and cassava that interfere with the utilization of iodine or with thyroid function. An iodine deficiency prevents adequate amounts of thyroid hormones from being made. This causes the metabolic rate to slow, resulting in fatigue and weight gain. Because thyroid hormones are important in growth and development, a deficiency of them causes a number of other conditions that, along with goiter, are called iodine deficiency disorders. In children and adolescents, iodine deficiency impairs mental function and reduces intellectual capacity. In pregnant women, this deficiency increases the risk of spontaneous abortion and of a condi-

FIGURE 8.4 Women suffering from goiter stand with their children in a hospital in the Democratic Republic of the Congo in October 2006. Goiter is the enlargement of the thyroid gland due to a shortage of iodine in the diet.

tion called **cretinism** in the offspring. Cretinism is characterized by impaired mental development, deafness, and growth failure.

Thanks to the fortification of table salt with iodine, cretinism and goiter now occur rarely in North America. Iodine deficiency remains a world health problem but its incidence has decreased dramatically since 1993 when universal salt iodization was adopted. In the last decade, the number of countries where iodine deficiency is a public health problem has been cut in half, and it is estimated that 66% of all households worldwide have access to iodized salt.

High intakes of iodine can cause an enlargement of the thyroid gland that resembles goiter, so levels of fortification and supplementation should be monitored.

CHROMIUM

Wouldn't it be great if people could take a pill that would decrease body fat and increase the amount of muscle? The dietary supplement **chromium picolinate** claims to do just that. Chromium is needed for normal function of the hormone insulin. Insulin is needed for the uptake of glucose by cells and the synthesis of proteins, lipids, and glycogen. Insulin's role in stimulating protein synthesis has led to claims that chromium supplements will increase muscle mass. Unfortunately, studies of chromium picolinate have found that it has no beneficial effects on muscle strength, body composition, or weight loss.

When the amount of chromium is deficient, insulin cannot function as effectively and it takes more insulin to produce the same effects. Chromium deficiency therefore affects the body's ability to regulate blood glucose and causes diabetes-like symptoms such as elevated blood glucose and increased insulin levels. Deficiencies have been reported in patients who are fed intravenous solutions devoid of chromium and in malnourished children, but overt chromium deficiency is not a problem in the United States.

Dietary sources of chromium include liver, nuts, and whole grains. Refined grains such as white breads, pasta, and white rice are poor sources because chromium is lost in the milling process and not added back in enrichment. Chromium intake can be increased by cooking in stainless steel cookware because chromium leaches from the steel into the food.

FLUORIDE

Fluoride is added to toothpaste because it helps prevent cavities. Fluoride consumed in the diet also helps prevent tooth decay. During tooth formation, it is incorporated into the enamel crystals of teeth, making them more resistant to the acid that causes decay. Fluoride has its greatest effect on cavity prevention early in life, during maximum tooth development (up to the age of 13), but it has also been shown to have beneficial effects throughout life. Fluoride contained in the saliva prevents cavities by reducing the amount of acid produced by bacteria, inhibiting the acid from dissolving tooth enamel, and increasing enamel re-mineralization

ENOUGH, BUT NOT TOO MUCH

In 1901, Dr. Fredrick McKay, a dentist in Colorado, noticed that many of his patients had stained, pitted teeth. The locals called the condition "Colorado brown stain." McKay believed that the condition was caused by something in the water. Analysis of water samples revealed that the local water supply contained high levels of fluoride; the condition was given the name fluorosis. Studies were conducted to determine how prevalent this condition was. When the prevalence of fluorosis was compared to the prevalence of cavities, it was discovered that children with fluorosis had fewer cavities. By examining the effects of different levels, it was determined that at the right dose, fluoride could prevent cavities without causing fluorosis. Studies conducted to stop the harm caused by too much fluoride had discovered the benefits of getting enough fluoride. This work helped to establish levels of water fluoridation that are safe but effective for preventing tooth decay.

after acid exposure. Fluoride is also incorporated into bone and is important for bone health.

Because fluoride is so important for dental health, it has been added to municipal water supplies since the 1940s. Today, over half of the population of the United States lives in communities with fluoridated drinking water. Fluoridated water and fluoride added to toothpaste account for a large portion of the fluoride in our diet. Natural sources of dietary fluoride include tea and marine fish consumed with their bones.

Excess intakes of fluoride can cause mottled teeth in children and extremely high doses can be deadly. In fact, the label on toothpaste with fluoride carries a warning that if more toothpaste is accidentally swallowed than used for brushing, professional help or a poison control center should be contacted immediately.

MOLYBDENUM

Molybdenum is needed to activate enzymes that are involved in the metabolism of sulfur-containing amino acids, nitrogen-containing compounds present in DNA and RNA, uric acid production, and the detoxification of other compounds. It is consumed in milk, milk products, organ meats, breads, cereals, and legumes. Deficiency is rare but has been reported in individuals who are fed intravenous solutions lacking molybdenum for long periods of time.

REVIEW

Minerals are elements needed by the body to provide structure and regulation. The bioavailability of minerals depends on the needs of the body as well as interactions with other constituents in the diet. The electrolytes sodium, potassium, and chloride are needed for fluid balance and nerve conduction. A high-sodium diet may contribute to hypertension. Calcium is needed for nerve transmission and muscle contraction and, along with phosphorus, forms the hard mineral deposits in bones and teeth. Too little calcium contributes to osteoporosis. Magnesium is also important for bone health and is a cofactor for enzymes involved in providing energy from carbohydrates, fat, and protein. Iron is part of hemoglobin, which transports oxygen in the blood, and it is a component of a number of proteins that are needed for energy metabolism. Iron deficiency anemia is common in the United States and around the world. Copper is needed for iron transport, connective tissue health, and antioxidant protection. Zinc is needed for tissue growth and repair, immune function, and antioxidant protection. Manganese is needed for the activity of a number of enzymes, including one involved in antioxidant defenses. Selenium is also needed for the activity of an antioxidant enzyme system. Iodine is a component of the thyroid hormones that regulate metabolic rate, growth, and development. Chromium is needed for the action of insulin. Fluoride is important for strong tooth enamel. Molybdenum is a coenzyme important in amino acid metabolism.

9

CHOOSING A HEALTHY DIET

Knowing what nutrients are and how much of each is recommended for optimal health is important. However, this information is not always helpful in choosing a healthy diet. Because of the wide variety of foods available today, there are many combinations of foods that make up a healthy diet. Virtually any food can be part of a healthy diet as long as it is balanced with other food choices throughout the day or week to meet but not exceed dietary needs.

WHAT IS A HEALTHY DIET?

A healthy diet provides the right number of calories to keep your weight in the desirable range; the proper balance of carbohydrates, protein, and fat choices; plenty of water; and sufficient but not excessive amounts of essential vitamins and minerals. How this translates into specific food choices depends on individual needs and preferences, but in general, a healthy diet is rich in whole grains, fruits, and vegetables; contains the right types of fats; and is low in added sugars. Choosing this diet does not mean people need to give up their favorite foods. But it does require them to think about the variety and balance of foods.

Variety is important to a healthy diet because different foods provide different nutrients. Following the recommendations of MyPyramid can provide a healthy variety of foods and, hence, nutrients. Making a variety of choices from within each food group is as important as choosing the right amounts from each food group. For example, strawberries are a fruit that provides vitamin C but little vitamin A, whereas apricots are a good a source of vitamin A, but provide less vitamin C. A diet that includes only strawberries will provide plenty of vitamin C, but may be lacking in vitamin A.

Balance is also part of a healthy diet. Balancing the diet means selecting foods that complement each other. This requires considering a food's nutrient density. Foods that are low in nutrient density, such as baked goods, snack foods, and sodas, should be balanced with nutrient-dense choices, such as salads, fruit, vegetables, and low-fat dairy products. A meal that consists of a burger, fries, and a soda, can be balanced by eating a salad, brown rice, and chicken at the next meal.

A varied diet that balances nutrient-poor choices with nutrient-dense ones can help most people meet their nutrient needs. For those who have increased needs or limited food choices, fortified foods are available. These foods contain added nutrients and include products such as calcium-fortified orange juice and iron-fortified breakfast cereals. In some cases, vitamin and mineral supplements can be helpful, but these should be used with caution to avoid consuming a toxic amount.

MAINTAINING A HEALTHY WEIGHT

A healthy body weight is associated with health and longevity. Maintaining a healthy weight means matching the calories you consume in your diet with the energy you expend to stay alive and active. Unfortunately, many Americans today consume more they expend and as a result gain more weight than is healthy.

ining a healthy lifestyle involves consuming a healthy diet participating in the right amount and kinds of physical activity. The most recent public health recommendations advise adults to get at least 150 minutes of moderately intense physical activity each week or 75 minutes a week of vigorous activity. This amount will reduce the risk of many of the chronic diseases that are common among Americans today. Moderate exercise is equivalent in effort to walking briskly and vigorous activity is equivalent in effort to running or jogging. Unfortunately, over three-quarters of all Americans are not meeting this guideline; this means that over 50 million people in the United States are at a significantly

TABLE 9.1 CALCULATING YOUR CALORIE NEEDS

- Determine your weight in kilograms (kg) and your height in meters (m)

  Weight in kg = weight in pounds/ 2.2 pounds per kg

  Height in meters = height in inches x 0.0254 inches per m

  For example: 160 pounds (lbs) = 160 lbs/2.2 lbs/kg = 72.7 kg

  5 feet 9 inches (in) = 69 in x 0.0254 in/m = 1.75 m

- Estimate your physical activity level and find your Physical Activity (PA) value in the table below.

  For example, if you are an active 18-year-old boy, your PA value is 1.26.

Life Stage	Physical Activity Value (PA)			
Activity Level	Sedentary	Low Active	Active	Very Active
Boys 3–18 yrs	1	1.13	1.26	1.42
Girls 3–18 yrs	1	1.16	1.31	1.56
Men	1	1.11	1.25	1.48
Women	1	1.12	1.27	1.45

increased risk of chronic health problems due to inactivity. Learning to choose foods wisely and to incorporate exercise into your daily routine can help you live a long and healthy life.

How Many Calories Do You Need?

The number of calories that individuals need depends on how many calories their bodies use. The body needs energy to stay alive, to keep the heart beating, the kidneys working, and the body warm. It needs energy to digest food and process the nutrients contained in the food. It also needs energy to fuel activity. A person's calorie needs can be estimated by calculating his or her estimated energy requirement (EER) using an equation that takes into account age, gender, height, weight, and activity level.

TABLE 9.1 **CALCULATING YOUR CALORIE NEEDS**
(continued)

- Use the appropriate EER prediction equation below to find your EER:
  For example: if you are an active 18-year-old male who weighs
    72.7 kg and is 1.75 m tall
  EER = 88.5 − (61.9 x 18) + 1.26 [(26.7 x 72.7) + (903 x 1.75)] + 25
    = 3,436 cal/day

Life Stage	EER Prediction Equation
Boys 9–18 yr	EER = 88.5 − (61.9 x age in yrs) + PA [(26.7 x weight in kg) + (903 x height in m)] + 25
Girls 9–18 yr	EER = 135.3 − (30.8 x age in yrs) + PA [(10.0 x weight in kg) + (934 x height in m)] + 25
Men ≥19 yr	EER = 662 − (9.53 x age in yrs) + PA [(15.91 x weight in kg) + (539.6 x height in m)]
Women ≥19 yr	EER = 354 − (6.91 x age in yrs) + PA [(9.36 x weight in kg) + (726 x height in m)]

To calculate a person's EER, his or her activity level must be estimated. For example, a "sedentary" individual is one who does not participate in any activity beyond that required for daily independent living, such as housework, homework, and yard work. To be in the "low active" category, an adult weighing 154 pounds (70 kg) would need to expend an amount of energy equivalent to walking about 2 miles at a rate of 3 to 4 miles per hour in addition to the activities of daily living. To be "active," this adult would need to perform daily exercise equivalent to walking at least 4 miles per day at this rate, and to be "very active," he or she would need to perform the equivalent of walking at least 10.3 miles per day at this rate in addition to the activities of daily living. Once the activity level has been estimated, the calorie needs can be calculated by using the appropriate physical activity (PA) value and equations in Table 9.1.

What Is a Healthy Weight for You?

The current standard for body weight is **body mass index**, or **BMI**. In general, people with a BMI within this range have the fewest health risks. BMI is a ratio of weight to height calculated by the following mathematical equation:

$$BMI = \text{weight in kg}/(\text{height in m})^2 \text{ or,}$$
$$BMI = \text{weight in pounds}/(\text{height in inches})^2 \times 703.$$

For example, someone who is 6 feet (72 inches) tall and weighs 180 pounds (82 kg) has a body mass index of 24.4 kg/m^2 (180 lbs/72 in^2 x 703). A healthy body weight is defined as a BMI between 18.5 and 24.9 kg/m^2 for individuals who are over the age of 20. Underweight is defined as a body mass index of less than 18.5 kg/m^2; overweight is defined as 25 to 29.9 kg/m^2; and obese is 30 kg/m^2 or greater. A BMI of 40 kg/m^2 or over is classified as extreme or morbid obesity. Because children and adolescents are still growing, these BMI ranges are not appropriate, so a healthy BMI for a child is defined by where the measurement falls on a BMI versus age growth chart (see the appendices). A BMI from the 5th to just below the 85th percentile is considered healthy. If the child's BMI is below the 5th percentile, he or she is considered underweight. A

BMI from the 85th to just below the 95th percentiles is considered overweight and a BMI at the 95th percentile or above is considered obese.

A healthy body weight also considers body composition, that is the proportion of fat versus lean tissue that make up the body. In general, women have more stored body fat than men and older adults have more body fat and less muscle than younger adults. For young adult women, the desirable amount of body fat is 21% to 32% of total weight; in adult men, the desirable amount is 8% to 19%.

An Obesity Epidemic

Do you weigh more than you would like? You are not alone. In the United States today, 66% of adults are either **overweight** or **obese**. This percentage has increased dramatically over the past 40 to 50 years (Figure 9.1). In 1960, 13.4% of American adults were obese; by 1990, about 23% were obese; and today, 32% of Americans are obese. The rise in obesity has been referred to as an "obesity epidemic." It affects both men and women and spans every age group and culture in the nation. Sixteen percent of U.S. children and adolescents ages 2 through 19 are obese.

Why are people getting fatter? The simple answer is that we are eating more calories than we are burning. When the number of calories we eat is equal to the number we expend, our weight remains stable. When we eat less than we expend, we lose weight, and when we eat more than we expend, we get fatter. One reason people in the United States today are eating more than they were 40 years ago is that a huge variety of tasty, affordable food is available 24 hours a day in supermarkets, fast-food restaurants, and all-night convenience marts. Another reason is that food portions are bigger. The portions we are offered in stores and restaurants have increased dramatically over the past few decades (Figure 9.2). When more food is placed in front of them, people eat more.

Another reason our energy balance is out of balance is that we are burning fewer calories in our daily lives. We ride to work in automobiles rather than walking or biking, we take the elevator instead of the stairs, and we use riding lawn mowers rather than push mowers. Many schools have reduced or even eliminated

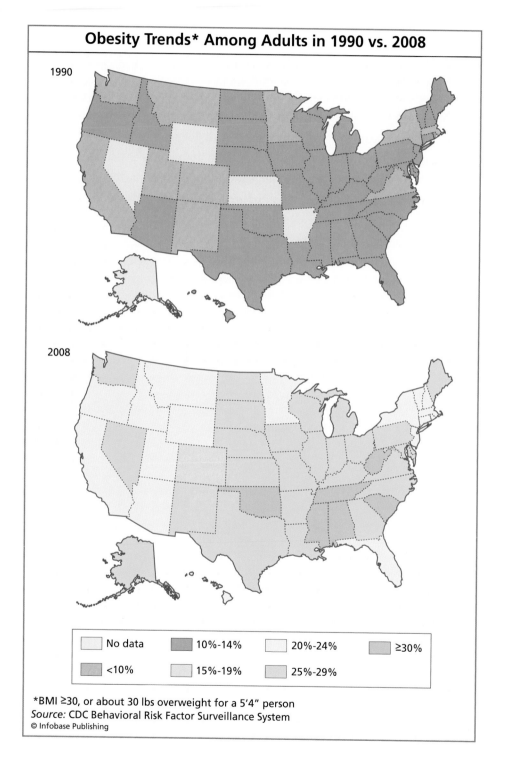

Obesity Trends* Among Adults in 1990 vs. 2008

1990

2008

| | No data | | 10%–14% | | 20%–24% | | ≥30% |
| | <10% | | 15%–19% | | 25%–29% | |

*BMI ≥30, or about 30 lbs overweight for a 5'4" person
Source: CDC Behavioral Risk Factor Surveillance System
© Infobase Publishing

physical education programs and our leisure time is spent sitting in front of televisions, video games, and computers (Table 9.2).

Even small changes in the balance between energy intake and energy expenditure could make a big difference in slowing the increase in obesity within the population. It has been estimated that a population-wide shift in energy balance of only 100 calories a day would prevent weight gain in 90% of the population. This means that people would need to eat 100 calories less per day or burn 100 calories more per day or some combination of the two. One hundred calories is the equivalent of walking for an extra 15 minutes a day or eating one small cookie instead of three.

BALANCING CARBOHYDRATES, FAT, AND PROTEIN

It's impossible to decrease the amount of fat in the diet without increasing the amount of carbohydrates or protein. Likewise, cutting down on carbohydrates means increasing the amount of fat or protein. Because these nutrients provide the calories needed to stay alive and healthy, reducing the intake of one means increasing the others in order to meet the body's energy needs. The recommendations of the DRIs recognize this by suggesting ranges of healthy intake: For adults, this mean intakes of 45% to 60% of calories from carbohydrates, 20% to 35% of calories as fat, and 10% to 35% of calories as protein. Within these ranges, there is no one magic combination of carbohydrate, fat, and protein that provides the optimal diet for everyone. You can choose a pattern that suits your personal preferences and health needs. For example, if you do not eat meat, your dietary pattern will probably be at the high

(opposite) **FIGURE 9.1** The number of Americans who are classified as obese or overweight has increased dramatically since 1990. Obesity affects men and women of all different ages and ethnicities.

NOT JUST AN AMERICAN PROBLEM

Obesity is not only a problem in the United States. It's a problem around the world as well. The term *globesity* has been used to describe the growing global obesity epidemic. Worldwide, there are approximately 1.6 billion adults who are overweight, and 400 million who are obese. The World Health Organization projects that by the year 2015, approximately 2.3 billion adults will be overweight and more than 700 million will be obese. Overweight and obesity were once considered problems only in high-income countries, but they are now also on the rise in low- and middle-income countries, particularly in cities. In many countries, the incidence of underweight from consumption of too few calories exists side by side with overweight from the consumption of more calories than are needed.

end of the recommended carbohydrate intake and at the low end of the range for protein. If you prefer a diet high in meat, you may choose one lower in carbohydrates and higher in protein. It is not just the amounts of these nutrients but the types of carbohydrates, fats, and proteins that affect your diet and your health.

Un-refining Carbohydrates

A healthy diet not only provides enough carbohydrates, but the right types of carbohydrates. Following the recommendations of the Dietary Guidelines and MyPyramid can help choose a diet that is based on whole grains, fruits, and vegetables, and that contains limited amounts of added sugars. The key is to choose carbohydrate sources that are less refined. Refining tends to add sugar, salt, and fat, while it removes fiber, vitamins, minerals and phytochemicals. With this in mind, fresh blueberries are better than a blueberry pie, fresh tomatoes are better than ketchup, and whole-wheat bread is better than white bread.

The ingredient list on food labels can be helpful in choosing foods that are low in added sugar and made from whole grains.

Since ingredients are listed in order of their prominence by weight, if a sweetener appears close to the beginning of the list, it is a clue that the food is high in added sugar. Products that list whole wheat or rolled oats as the first ingredient contain mostly these whole grains. Whole grains are high in fiber and the total amount of fiber in a serving of the food is listed in the Nutrition Facts part of the label.

Figuring Out Fats

You do not have to eat a diet with only 20% fat to be healthy. A diet with 35% fat, or 40% for children and teens, can be just as healthy if the types of fat are chosen wisely. The goal is to choose fats that are mono- or polyunsaturated and that will minimize your consumption of saturated fat, cholesterol, and trans fat. MyPyramid distinguishes

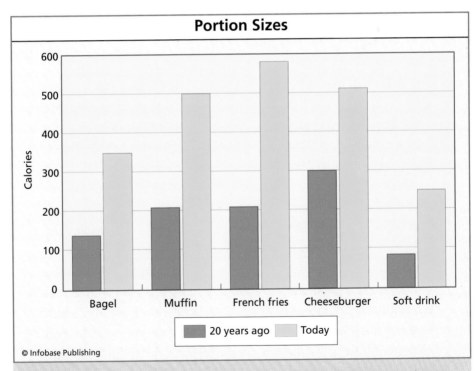

© Infobase Publishing

FIGURE 9.2 In the past few decades, food portions have grown larger, causing people to consume more calories. This factor, combined with lack of exercise and poor eating habits, has contributed to the increasing number of obese and overweight Americans.

IS THAT A SERVING OR A PORTION?

On a hot day, a bottle of ice tea or fruit juice may be just what you need to cool off. The label on that bottle of tea or juice may say that a serving has only 100 calories. Take a closer look. The serving size is 8 ounces and the bottle is 20 ounces. So the portion of tea you are about to drink will be a lot more than 100 calories. People tend to eat in units: one cookie, one can, one bottle. You are unlikely to drink half the bottle and save the rest for later. Food manufacturers are required to use standard serving sizes on the label, but they are not required to package products according to these standards. Even if the package is clearly meant to contain multiple servings, your portion may not match the serving listed. For example, your one-cup bowl of granola for breakfast is probably about 4 servings, for a total of over 400 calories. Pasta is also a challenge when making calorie estimates because the 2-ounce serving size listed on the label refers to 2 ounces of dry pasta. What does 2 ounces of spaghetti look like once it is cooked? It is actually about a cup, so if you put 2 cups onto your plate, you are getting two servings providing 400 calories rather than the 200 calories listed on the box.

between solid and liquid fats, recommending that solid fats be limited. Solid fats are usually high in saturated fat and trans fat—fats that can raise blood cholesterol levels. Saturated fats are found in animal foods and trans fat is found in products containing hydrogenated oils, such as solid margarines and shortening. Check the Nutrition Facts portion of the label to look for products low in trans fat, saturated fat, and cholesterol. Liquid fats are typically mono- and polyunsaturated fats; these do not cause an increase in blood cholesterol. Olive, canola, and peanut oils are high in monounsaturated fat; other vegetable oils are high in polyunsaturated fat.

Picking Your Proteins

Most Americans eat plenty of protein. A diet that meets the recommendations of MyPyramid provides about 70 grams of protein—

more than enough to meet most people's needs. Which proteins are picked, however, may have as much impact on fat and carbohydrate intake as it does on meeting protein needs. Animal sources of protein provide high-quality protein, but they are often also high in saturated fat and cholesterol. The saturated fat consumed in these high-quality proteins can be reduced by trimming the fat off the meat and broiling or grilling the meat to allow the fat to drip off the food. Getting some protein from whole grains and legumes helps keep the diet low in saturated fat and cholesterol and high in fiber.

Choosing nuts as a protein source adds monounsaturated fat, omega-3 polyunsaturated fatty acids, and fiber. Choosing fish adds omega-3 polyunsaturated fatty acids.

GETTING VITAMINS AND MINERALS

Most foods naturally contain some vitamins and minerals. The cooking, storage, and processing of food can cause some vitamins

TABLE 9.2 IF YOU EAT MORE, EXERCISE MORE

If you choose...	Then add this to your day . . .
A quarter-pounder with cheese instead of a plain burger	30 minutes of racquetball
Breaded chicken sandwich instead of a grilled chicken sandwich	A 30-minute walk
Large French fries instead of small fries	An hour-long bike ride
Nachos with cheese sauce instead of baked tortilla chips and salsa	A 30-minute swim
A slice of stuffed crust pepperoni pizza instead of a slice of thin crust vegetarian pizza	A half hour of tennis

and minerals to be lost. Other types of food processing can add vitamins and minerals. Vitamin and mineral needs can be met by a diet that is high in unrefined foods. Vitamins and minerals can also be obtained by choosing fortified foods or using vitamin and mineral supplements.

The Benefits of Whole Foods

The foods we eat provide a huge variety of colors, aromas, and flavors as well as a boundless combination of nutrients. Whole foods, meaning those that are least refined and processed, are often the best way to meet vitamin and mineral needs. For instance, whole-grain breads are a good source of iron, selenium, zinc, copper, and many B vitamins. When wheat is refined to make the white flour used to bake white bread, many of those nutrients are lost. Processing also reduces nutrient density by adding calories from sugar and fat. For example, turning potatoes into potato chips adds fat and salt and removes the fiber-rich skins; turning strawberries into strawberry jam adds sugar; and turning milk into ice cream increases the amount of fat and sugar.

Another benefit of whole foods is that they also provide other health-promoting substances such as phytochemicals. Foods high in phytochemicals often provide health benefits that extend beyond basic nutrition. Research studies have repeatedly identified a relationship between diets that are high in plant foods, and thus high in phytochemicals, and a reduction in the incidence of chronic disease.

Fortified Foods

The addition of nutrients to foods is called fortification. Some food fortification is mandatory. For example, in the United States, the FDA mandates that refined grain products be fortified with the vitamins thiamin, niacin, riboflavin, and folic acid and the mineral iron. Fortification is also a marketing tool that food manufacturers use to make products more appealing to their customers and increase sales. For example, breakfast cereals are often fortified with so many vitamins that they resemble a multivitamin supplement. Foods fortified with nutrients, such as calcium and iron, which are present at low levels in the American diet, can make it easier for many people to consume enough of these nutrients. But some foods are fortified with large amounts of nutrients; therefore, when choosing fortified foods, it is important to be sure the intake does not exceed the UL for any nutrient.

Supplements Can Help or Hurt

Dietary supplements are another source of vitamins and minerals in the American diet. Although most individuals can meet their

HOW TO CHOOSE A DIETARY SUPPLEMENT

Is your supplement safe? Is it providing any benefits? Before you start taking any dietary supplements, ask yourself the following questions:

- **Why are you taking the supplement?** If you are taking it to ensure you receive enough of a certain nutrient, does it provide both vitamins and minerals? If you want to supplement specific nutrients, are they contained in the product?
- **Does it contain potentially toxic levels of any nutrient?** To find out, check Tables 7.1 and 8.1 to see if the amounts of any vitamins or minterals in your supplement exceed the UL.
- **Does it contain ingredients other than vitamins and minerals?** If so, are these known to be safe?
- **Do you have a medical condition that recommends against certain nutrients or other ingredients?** If so, be sure your supplement does not contain these.
- **Are you taking prescription medication with which the supplement may interact?** Check with your physician, dietitian, or pharmacist to help identify these interactions.
- **How much does it cost?** A high price tag does not always mean it is better. Compare costs and ingredients before you buy.

needs by consuming a varied, balanced diet, individuals who have increased needs, such as pregnant women, children, older adults, those whose intake is limited by dietary restrictions, and those whose absorption or utilization is limited by disease may need supplements to meet their needs. Consumers need to be aware, however, that supplements pose a toxicity risk. While it is difficult to consume a toxic amount of a vitamin by eating food, it is easy to take too large a dose in a supplement.

Many supplements that are available on the market today also contain substances that are not nutrients, such as herbs. Some of these are safe, but others may have side effects that outweigh any benefits they provide. Because the manufacture of dietary supplements is not strictly regulated and supplements may not be stringently tested for safety before they are marketed, supplements that are dangerous may be on the market for years before enough evidence has accumulated to remove them. Supplements should always be taken with caution.

REVIEW

A healthy diet is one that provides the right number of calories to keep your weight in the healthy range; a balance of carbohydrate, protein, and fat choices; plenty of water; and sufficient but not excessive amounts of essential vitamins and minerals. Maintaining a healthy weight means balancing the calories you consume in your diet with the amount of energy you burn to stay alive and moving. Calorie needs can be estimated by using the EER equations. A healthy body weight is a weight that is associated with health and longevity. Unfortunately, many Americans are currently overweight or obese. Many different dietary patterns are healthy, but, in general, a healthy diet should include plenty of unrefined grains, fruits, and vegetables; be limited in saturated fat, trans fat, and cholesterol; and provide adequate protein. Vitamin and mineral needs can be met by consuming natural sources of vitamins and minerals as well as by using fortified foods and supplements. The risk of nutrient toxicity is increased when supplements that contain large or imbalanced amounts of nutrients are consumed.

APPENDIX A

DIETARY REFERENCE INTAKES

ACCEPTABLE MACRONUTRIENT DISTRIBUTION RANGES (AMDR) FOR HEALTHY DIETS AS A PERCENTAGE OF ENERGY						
Age	Carbohydrates	Added Sugars	Total Fat	Linoleic Acid	α-Linolenic Acid	Protein
1–3 years old	45–65	25	30–40	5–10	0.6–1.2	5–20
4–18 years old	45–65	25	25–35	5–10	0.6–1.2	10–30
≥ 19 years old	45–65	25	20–35	5–10	0.6–1.2	10–35

Source: Institute of Medicine, Food and Nutrition Board. "Dietary Reference Intakes for Energy, Carbohydrates, Fiber, Fat, Protein, and Amino Acids." Washington, D.C.: National Academies Press, 2002.

RECOMMENDED INTAKES OF VITAMINS FOR VARIOUS AGE GROUPS

Life Stage	Vit A (µg/day)	Vit C (mg/day)	Vit D (Cg/day)	Vit E (mg/day)	Vit K (µg/day)
Infants					
0–6 mo	400	40	5	4	2.0
7–12 mo	500	50	5	5	2.5
Children					
1–3 yrs	**300**	**15**	5	**6**	30
4–8 yrs	**400**	**25**	5	**7**	55
Males					
9–13 yrs	**600**	**45**	5	**11**	60
14–18 yrs	**900**	**75**	5	**15**	75
19–30 yrs	**900**	**90**	5	**15**	120
31–50 yrs	**900**	**90**	5	**15**	120
51–70 yrs	**900**	**90**	10	**15**	120
>70 yrs	**900**	**90**	15	**15**	120
Females					
9–13 yrs	**600**	**45**	5	**11**	60
14–18 yrs	**700**	**65**	5	**15**	75
19–30 yrs	**700**	**75**	5	**15**	90
31–50 yrs	**700**	**75**	5	**15**	90
51–70 yrs	**700**	**75**	10	**15**	90
>70 yrs	**700**	**75**	15	**15**	90
Pregnancy					
≤18 yrs	**750**	**80**	5	**15**	75
19–30 yrs	**770**	**85**	5	**15**	90
31–50 yrs	**770**	**85**	5	**15**	90
Lactation					
≤18 yrs	**1,200**	**115**	5	**19**	75
19–30 yrs	**1,300**	**120**	5	**19**	90
31–50 yrs	**1,300**	**120**	5	**19**	90

RECOMMENDED INTAKES OF VITAMINS
FOR VARIOUS AGE GROUPS (continued)

Life Stage	Thiamin (mg/day)	Riboflavin (mg/day)	Niacin (mg/day)	Vit B$_6$ (mg/day)	Folate (µg/day)
Infants					
0–6 mo	0.2	0.3	2	0.1	65
7–12 mo	0.3	0.4	4	0.3	80
Children					
1–3 yrs	**0.5**	**0.5**	**6**	**0.5**	**150**
4–8 yrs	**0.6**	**0.6**	**8**	**0.6**	**200**
Males					
9–13 yrs	**0.9**	**0.9**	**12**	**1.0**	**300**
14–18 yrs	**1.2**	**1.3**	**16**	**1.3**	**400**
19–30 yrs	**1.2**	**1.3**	**16**	**1.3**	**400**
31–50 yrs	**1.2**	**1.3**	**16**	**1.3**	**400**
51–70 yrs	**1.2**	**1.3**	**16**	**1.7**	**400**
>70 yrs	**1.2**	**1.3**	**16**	**1.7**	**400**
Females					
9–13 yrs	**0.9**	**0.9**	**12**	**1.0**	**300**
14–18 yrs	**1.0**	**1.0**	**14**	**1.2**	**400**
19–30 yrs	**1.1**	**1.1**	**14**	**1.3**	**400**
31–50 yrs	**1.1**	**1.1**	**14**	**1.3**	**400**
51–70 yrs	**1.1**	**1.1**	**14**	**1.5**	**400**
>70 yrs	**1.1**	**1.1**	**14**	**1.5**	**400**
Pregnancy					
≤18 yrs	**1.4**	**1.4**	**18**	**1.9**	**600**
19–30 yrs	**1.4**	**1.4**	**18**	**1.9**	**600**
31–50 yrs	**1.4**	**1.4**	**18**	**1.9**	**600**
Lactation					
≤18 yrs	**1.4**	**1.6**	**17**	**2.0**	**500**
19–30 yrs	**1.4**	**1.6**	**17**	**2.0**	**500**
31–50 yrs	**1.4**	**1.6**	**17**	**2.0**	**500**

(continues)

RECOMMENDED INTAKES OF VITAMINS FOR VARIOUS AGE GROUPS (continued)

Life Stage	Vit B$_{12}$ (µg/day)	Pantothenic Acid (mg/day)	Biotin Group (µg/day)	Choline* (mg/day)
Infants				
0–6 mo	0.4	1.7	5	125
7–12 mo	0.5	1.8	6	150
Children				
1–3 yrs	0.9	2	8	200
4–8 yrs	1.2	3	12	250
Males				
9–13 yrs	1.8	4	20	375
14–18 yrs	2.4	5	25	550
19–30 yrs	2.4	5	30	550
31–50 yrs	2.4	5	30	550
51–70 yrs	2.4	5	30	550
>70 yrs	2.4	5	30	550
Females				
9–13 yrs	1.8	4	20	375
14–18 yrs	2.4	5	25	400
19–30 yrs	2.4	5	30	425
31–50 yrs	2.4	5	30	425
51–70 yrs	2.4	5	30	425
>70 yrs	2.4	5	30	425
Pregnancy				
≤18 yrs	2.6	6	30	450
19–30 yrs	2.6	6	30	450
31–50 yrs	2.6	6	30	450
Lactation				
≤18 yrs	2.8	7	35	550
19–30 yrs	2.8	7	35	550
31–50 yrs	2.8	7	35	550

Note: This table presents Recommended Dietary Allowances (RDAs) in bold type and Adequate Intakes (AIs) in ordinary type.

* Not yet classified as a vitamin

Source: Adapted from Dietary Reference Intake Tables: The Complete Set. *Institute of Medicine, National Academy of Sciences. Available online at www.nap.edu.*

RECOMMENDED INTAKES OF SELECTED MINERALS FOR VARIOUS AGE GROUPS

Life Stage	Calcium (mg/day)	Chromium (µg/day)	Copper (µg/day)	Fluroide (mg/day)	Iodine (µg/day)
Infants					
0–6 mo	210	0.2	200	0.01	110
7–12 mo	270	5.5	220	0.5	130
Children					
1–3 yrs	500	11	**340**	0.7	**90**
4–8 yrs	800	15	**440**	1	**90**
Males					
9–13 yrs	1,300	25	**700**	2	**120**
14–18 yrs	1,300	35	**890**	3	**150**
19–30 yrs	1,000	35	**900**	4	**150**
31–50 yrs	1,000	35	**900**	4	**150**
51–70 yrs	1,200	30	**900**	4	**150**
>70 yrs	1,200	30	**900**	4	**150**
Females					
9–13 yrs	1,300	21	**700**	2	**120**
14–18 yrs	1,300	24	**890**	3	**150**
19–30 yrs	1,000	25	**900**	3	**150**
31–50 yrs	1,000	25	**900**	3	**150**
51–70 yrs	1,200	20	**900**	3	**150**
>70 yrs	1,200	20	**900**	3	**150**
Pregnancy					
≤18 yrs	1,300	29	**1,000**	3	**220**
19–30 yrs	1,000	30	**1,000**	3	**220**
31–50 yrs	1,000	30	**1,000**	3	**220**
Lactation					
≤18 yrs	1,300	44	**1,300**	3	**290**
19–30 yrs	1,000	45	**1,300**	3	**290**
31–50 yrs	1,000	45	**1,300**	3	**290**

(continues)

RECOMMENDED INTAKES OF SELECTED MINERALS FOR VARIOUS AGE GROUPS (continued)

Life Stage	Iron (mg/day)	Magnesium (mg/day)	Phosphorus (mg/day)	Selenium (µg/day)
Infants				
0–6 mo	0.27	30	100	15
7–12 mo	11	75	275	20
Children				
1–3 yrs	7	80	460	20
4–8 yrs	10	130	500	30
Males				
9–13 yrs	8	240	1,250	40
14–18 yrs	11	410	1,250	55
19–30 yrs	8	400	700	55
31–50 yrs	8	420	700	55
51–70 yrs	8	420	700	55
>70 yrs	8	420	700	55
Females				
9–13 yrs	8	240	1,250	40
14–18 yrs	15	360	1,250	55
19–30 yrs	18	310	700	55
31–50 yrs	18	320	700	55
51–70 yrs	8	320	700	55
>70 yrs	8	320	700	55
Pregnancy				
≤18 yrs	27	400	1,250	60
19–30 yrs	27	350	700	60
31–50 yrs	27	360	700	60
Lactation				
≤18 yrs	10	360	1,250	70
19–30 yrs	9	310	700	70
31–50 yrs	9	320	700	70

RECOMMENDED INTAKES OF SELECTED MINERALS FOR VARIOUS AGE GROUPS (continued)

Life Stage	Zinc (mg/day)	Sodium (g/day)	Chloride (g/day)	Potassium (g/day)
Infants				
0–6 mo	2	0.12	0.18	0.4
7–12 mo	**3**	0.37	0.57	0.7
Children				
1–3 yrs	**3**	1.0	1.5	3.0
4–8 yrs	**5**	1.2	1.9	3.8
Males				
9–13 yrs	**8**	1.5	2.3	4.5
14–18 yrs	**11**	1.5	2.3	4.7
19–30 yrs	**11**	1.5	2.3	4.7
31–50 yrs	**11**	1.5	2.3	4.7
51–70 yrs	**11**	1.3	2.0	4.7
>70 yrs	**11**	1.2	1.8	4.7
Females				
9–13 yrs	**8**	1.5	2.3	4.5
14–18 yrs	**9**	1.5	2.3	4.7
19–30 yrs	**8**	1.5	2.3	4.7
31–50 yrs	**8**	1.5	2.3	4.7
51–70 yrs	**8**	1.3	2.0	4.7
>70 yrs	**8**	1.2	1.8	4.7
Pregnancy				
≤18 yrs	**13**	1.5	2.3	4.7
19–30 yrs	**11**	1.5	2.3	4.7
31–50 yrs	**11**	1.5	2.3	4.7
Lactation				
≤18 yrs	**14**	1.5	2.3	5.1
19–30 yrs	**12**	1.5	2.3	5.1
31–50 yrs	**12**	1.5	2.3	5.1

Note: This table presents Recommended Dietary Allowances (RDAs) in bold type and Adequate Intakes (AIs) in ordinary type.

Source: Adapted from Dietary Reference Intake Tables: The Complete Set. *Institute of Medicine, National Academy of Sciences. Available online at www.nap.edu.*

APPENDIX B

HEALTHY BODY WEIGHTS
Body Mass Index (BMI)

Body mass index, or BMI, is the measurement of choice for determining health risks associated with body weight. BMI uses a mathematical formula that takes into account both a person's height and weight. BMI equals a person's weight in kilograms divided by height in meters squared ($BMI = kg/m^2$).

RISK OF ASSOCIATED DISEASE ACCORDING TO BMI AND WAIST SIZE FOR ADULTS			
BMI		Waist less than or equal to 40 in. (men) or 35 in. (women)	Waist greater than 40 in. (men) or 35 in. (women)
18.5 or less	Underweight	N/A	N/A
18.5–24.9	Normal	N/A	N/A
25.0–29.9	Overweight	Increased	High
30.0–34.9	Obese	High	Very High
35.0–39.9	Obese	Very High	Very High
40 or greater	Extremely Obese	Extremely High	Extremely High

Determining Your Body Mass Index (BMI)

To use the table on the following page, find the appropriate height in the left-hand column. Move across the row to the given weight. The number at the top of the column is the BMI for that height and weight. Then use the table above to determine how at risk you are for developing a weight-related disease.

BMI (kg/m²)	19	20	21	22	23	24	25	26	27	28	29	30	35	40
Height (in.)							Weight (lb)							
58	91	96	100	105	110	115	119	124	129	134	138	143	167	191
59	94	99	104	109	114	119	124	128	133	138	143	148	173	198
60	97	102	107	112	118	123	128	133	138	143	148	153	179	204
61	100	106	111	116	122	127	132	137	143	148	153	158	185	211
62	104	109	115	120	126	131	136	142	147	153	158	164	191	218
63	107	113	118	124	130	135	141	146	152	158	163	169	197	225
64	110	116	122	128	134	140	145	151	157	163	169	174	204	232
65	114	120	126	132	138	144	150	156	162	168	174	180	210	240
66	118	124	130	136	142	148	155	161	167	173	179	186	216	247
67	121	127	134	140	146	153	159	166	172	178	185	191	223	255
68	125	131	138	144	151	158	164	171	177	184	190	197	230	262
69	128	135	142	149	155	162	169	176	182	189	196	203	236	270
70	132	139	146	153	160	167	174	181	188	195	202	207	243	278
71	136	143	150	157	165	172	179	186	193	200	208	215	250	286
72	140	147	154	162	169	177	184	191	199	206	213	221	258	294
73	144	151	159	166	174	182	189	197	204	212	219	227	265	302
74	148	155	163	171	179	186	194	202	210	218	225	233	272	311
75	152	160	168	176	184	192	200	208	216	224	232	240	279	319
76	156	164	172	180	189	197	205	213	221	230	238	246	287	328

Source: Adapted from Partnership for Healthy Weight Management, http://www.consumer.gov/weightloss/bmi.htm.

BMI-FOR-AGE GROWTH CHARTS

2 to 20 years: Boys
Body mass index-for-age percentiles

NAME _____

RECORD # _____

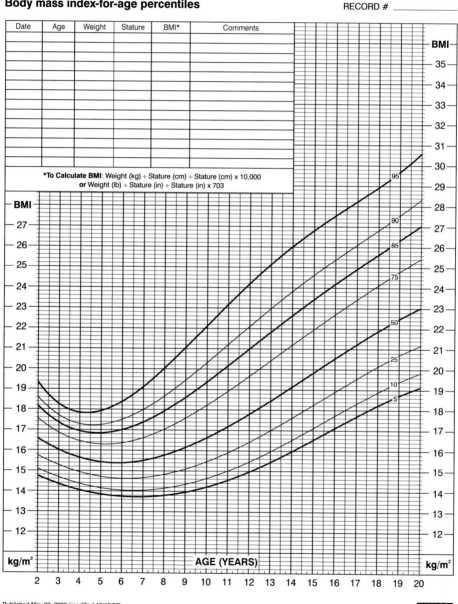

Date	Age	Weight	Stature	BMI*	Comments

*To Calculate BMI: Weight (kg) ÷ Stature (cm) ÷ Stature (cm) x 10,000
or Weight (lb) ÷ Stature (in) ÷ Stature (in) x 703

AGE (YEARS)

Published May 30, 2000 (modified 10/16/00).
SOURCE: Developed by the National Center for Health Statistics in collaboration with
the National Center for Chronic Disease Prevention and Health Promotion (2000).
http://www.cdc.gov/growthcharts

CDC

SAFER·HEALTHIER·PEOPLE™

2 to 20 years: Girls
Body mass index-for-age percentiles

NAME _____

RECORD # _____

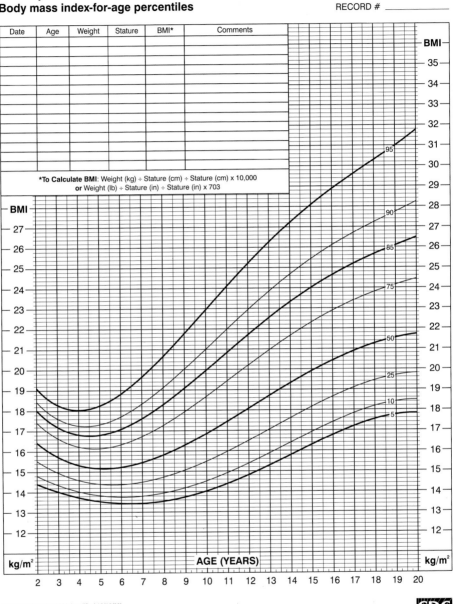

Date	Age	Weight	Stature	BMI*	Comments

*To Calculate **BMI**: Weight (kg) ÷ Stature (cm) ÷ Stature (cm) x 10,000
or Weight (lb) ÷ Stature (in) ÷ Stature (in) x 703

AGE (YEARS)

Published May 30, 2000 (modified 10/16/00).
SOURCE: Developed by the National Center for Health Statistics in collaboration with
the National Center for Chronic Disease Prevention and Health Promotion (2000).
http://www.cdc.gov/growthcharts

CDC

SAFER·HEALTHIER·PEOPLE™

APPENDIX C

BLOOD VALUES OF NUTRITIONAL RELEVANCE

Red blood cells	
Men	4.6–6.2 million/mm³
Women	4.2–5.2 million/mm³
White blood cells	5,000–10,000/mm³
Calcium	9–11 mg/100 mL
Iron	
Men	75–175 µg/100 mL
Women	65–165 µg/100 mL
Zinc	0.75–1.4 µg/mL
Potassium	3.5–5.0 mEq/L
Sodium	136–145 mEq/L
Vitamin A	20–80 µg/100 mL
Vitamin B_{12}	200–800 pg/100 mL
Vitamin C	0.6–2.0 mg/100 mL
Folate	2–20 ng/mL
pH	7.35–7.45
Total protein	6.6–8.0 g/100 mL
Albumin	3.0–4.0 g/100 mL
Cholesterol	less than 200 mg/100 mL
Glucose	60–100 mg/100 mL blood, 70–120 mg/100 mL serum

Source: Handbook of Clinical Dietetics, *American Dietetic Association (New Haven, Conn.: Yale University Press, 1981); and Committee on Dietetics of the Mayo Clinic,* Mayo Clinic Diet Manual *(Philadelphia: W. B. Saunders Company, 1981), pp. 275–277.*

APPENDIX D

USDA'S MYPYRAMID

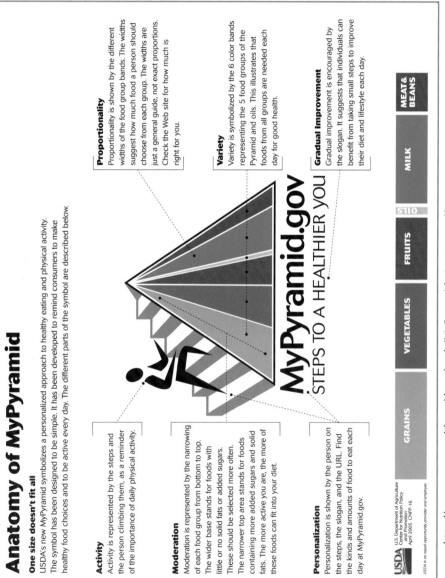

Anatomy of MyPyramid

One size doesn't fit all

USDA's new MyPyramid symbolizes a personalized approach to healthy eating and physical activity. The symbol has been designed to be simple. It has been developed to remind consumers to make healthy food choices and to be active every day. The different parts of the symbol are described below.

Activity
Activity is represented by the steps and the person climbing them, as a reminder of the importance of daily physical activity.

Moderation
Moderation is represented by the narrowing of each food group from bottom to top. The wider base stands for foods with little or no solid fats or added sugars. These should be selected more often. The narrower top area stands for foods containing more added sugars and solid fats. The more active you are, the more of these foods can fit into your diet.

Personalization
Personalization is shown by the person on the steps, the slogan, and the URL. Find the kinds and amounts of food to eat each day at MyPyramid.gov.

Proportionality
Proportionality is shown by the different widths of the food group bands. The widths suggest how much food a person should choose from each group. The widths are just a general guide, not exact proportions. Check the Web site for how much is right for you.

Variety
Variety is symbolized by the 6 color bands representing the 5 food groups of the Pyramid and oils. This illustrates that foods from all groups are needed each day for good health.

Gradual Improvement
Gradual improvement is encouraged by the slogan. It suggests that individuals can benefit from taking small steps to improve their diet and lifestyle each day.

MyPyramid.gov
STEPS TO A HEALTHIER YOU

GRAINS   VEGETABLES   FRUITS   MILK   MEAT & BEANS

USDA U.S. Department of Agriculture
Center for Nutrition Policy and Promotion
April 2005 CNPP-16

USDA is an equal opportunity provider and employer.

Source: http://www.mypyramid.gov/downloads/MyPyramid_Anatomy.pdf.

GLOSSARY

Absorption The process of taking substances into the body

Added refined sugar Sugar that is refined from its original food source and added to food

Adenosine triphosphate (ATP) The high-energy molecule used by the body to perform energy-requiring activities

Adequate Intakes (AIs) Intakes recommended by the DRIs that should be used as a goal when no RDA exists; these values are an approximation of the average nutrient intake that appears to sustain a desired indicator of health.

Adipose tissue Tissue found under the skin and around body organs that is composed of fat-storing cells

Aerobic metabolism Metabolism in the presence of oxygen that produces carbon dioxide, water, and ATP

Aldosterone A hormone that increases sodium reabsorption by the kidney and therefore enhances water retention

Alpha-carotene (α-carotene) A carotenoid found in leafy green vegetables, carrots, and squash that provides some vitamin A activity

Alpha-linolenic acid (α-linolenic) An essential omega-3 fatty acid found in vegetable oils

Alpha-tocopherol (α-tocopherol) A form of tocopherol that provides vitamin E activity in humans

Amino acids The building blocks of proteins; each contains a carbon atom bound to a hydrogen atom, an amino group, an acid group, and a side chain.

Amylase An enzyme secreted by the salivary glands that breaks down starch

Anaerobic glycolysis or **anaerobic metabolism** Metabolism in the absence of oxygen, also called glycolysis

Angiotensin II A protein that causes blood vessel walls to constrict and stimulates the release of the hormone aldosterone

Antibodies   Proteins produced by cells of the immune system that destroy or deactivate foreign substances in the body

Anticoagulant   A substance that delays or prevents blood clotting

Antidiuretic hormone (ADH)   A hormone secreted by the pituitary gland that increases the amount of water reabsorbed by the kidney and, therefore, retained in the body

Antioxidant   A substance that is able to neutralize reactive molecules and, hence, reduce the amount of oxidative damage that occurs

Ariboflavinosis   A deficiency of the vitamin riboflavin

Arteries   Vessels that carry blood away from the heart

Ascorbate or ascorbic acid   The chemical term for vitamin C

Atherosclerosis   A type of cardiovascular disease that involves the buildup of fatty material in the artery walls

ATP   See adenosine triphosphate.

Atrophic gastritis   An inflammation of the stomach that causes a reduction in stomach acid

Avidin   A protein in raw egg whites that binds with biotin and prevents its absorption

Beriberi   A disease resulting from a deficiency of thiamin

Beta-carotene (ß-carotene)   A carotenoid that has more provitamin A activity than other carotenoids; it also acts as an antioxidant.

Beta-cryptoxanthin (ß-cryptoxanthin)   A carotenoid found in papaya, red bell peppers, and squash that can provide some vitamin A activity

Bile   A substance made in the liver and stored in the gallbladder; it is released into the small intestine to aid in fat digestion and absorption.

Bile acids   Emulsifiers present in bile that are synthesized by the liver from cholesterol

Bioavailability   A general term that refers to how well a nutrient can be absorbed and used by the body

Blood pressure   The amount of force exerted by the blood against the artery walls

Body Mass Index (BMI)   The current standard for assessing body weight; a BMI between 18.5 and 24.9 kg/m^2 is considered healthy for adults.

Bran   The protective outer layers of whole grains; it is a concentrated source of dietary fiber.

Buffer   A substance that reacts with an acid or base by picking up or releasing hydrogen ions to prevent changes in acidity

Calcitonin   A hormone secreted by the thyroid gland that reduces blood calcium levels

Calorie   The amount of heat needed to raise the temperature of one gram of water by 1°C; it is commonly used to refer to a kilocalorie, which is 1,000 calories.

Capillaries   Small, thin-walled blood vessels where the exchange of gases and nutrients between blood and cells occurs

Cardiovascular disease   Any disease affecting the heart and blood vessels

Carotenoids   Natural pigments synthesized by plants and many microorganisms; they give yellow and red-orange fruits and vegetables their color.

Cell differentiation   Structural and functional changes that cause cells to mature into specialized cells

Cell membrane   The membrane that surrounds the cell contents

Cells   The basic structural and functional units of plant and animal life

Cellular respiration   The reactions that break down glucose, fatty acids, and amino acids in the presence of oxygen to produce carbon dioxide, water, and energy in the form of ATP

Chemical bonds   Forces that hold atoms together

Cholesterol   A lipid made only by animal cells that consists of multiple chemical rings

Chromium picolinate   A form of chromium supplement that is sold to promote fat loss and an increase in muscle mass

Chylomicrons   Lipoproteins that transport lipids from the mucosal cells of the intestine to other body cells

Citric acid cycle   Also known as the Krebs cycle or the tricarboxylic acid cycle, this is the stage of respiration in which acetyl-CoA is broken down into 2 molecules of carbon dioxide.

Cobalamin   The chemical term for vitamin B_{12}

Coenzymes   Small nonprotein, organic molecules that act as carriers of electrons or atoms in metabolic reactions and are necessary for the proper functioning of many enzymes

Cofactor   A mineral or a coenzyme required for enzyme activity

Collagen   The major protein in connective tissue

Colon   The largest portion of the large intestine

Complex carbohydrates   Carbohydrates composed of sugar molecules linked together in straight or branching chains; they include starches and fibers.

Cretinism   A condition resulting from poor maternal iodine intake during pregnancy that causes stunted growth and poor mental development in offspring

Cytoplasm   The cellular material outside the nucleus that is contained by the cell membrane

Daily Value   A nutrient reference value used on food labels to help consumers see how foods fit into their overall diets

DASH diet (Dietary Approaches to Stop Hypertension)   A dietary pattern that lowers blood pressure; it is high in fruits, vegetables, and low-fat dairy products and, therefore, high in potassium, magnesium, calcium, and fiber, and low in saturated fat and cholesterol.

Dehydration   A deficiency of water

Dental caries   The decay and deterioration of teeth caused by acid produced when bacteria on the teeth metabolize carbohydrates

Deoxyribonucleic acid (DNA)   The genetic material found in the cell nucleus that codes for the synthesis of proteins

Diabetes or diabetes mellitus   A disease caused by either insufficient insulin production or decreased sensitivity of cells to insulin; it results in elevated blood glucose levels.

Dietary References Intakes (DRIs)   A set of reference values for the intake of nutrients and food components that can be used for planning and assessing the diets of healthy people in the United States and Canada

Dietary Supplements   Products taken to supplement nutrients or other substances in the diet

Digestion The process of breaking food into components small enough to be absorbed into the body

Disaccharide A sugar formed by linking two monosaccharides

Diverticulosis A condition in which sacs or pouches called diverticula form in the wall of the large intestine. When these become inflamed, the condition is called diverticulitis.

Docosahexaenoic acid (DHA) An omega-3 fatty acid found in fish oils

DNA See *deoxyribonucleic acid.*

Eicosanoids Regulatory molecules that can be synthesized from omega-3 and omega-6 fatty acids

Eicosapentaenoic acid (EPA) An omega-3 fatty acid found in fish oils

Electrolytes Positively and negatively charged ions that conduct an electrical current in solution; the term commonly refers to sodium, potassium, and chloride.

Electron transport chain The final stage of cellular respiration in which electrons are passed down a chain of molecules to oxygen to form water and produce ATP

Elements Substances that cannot be broken down into products with different properties

Empty calories Refers to foods that contribute energy but few nutrients

Emulsifiers Substances that allow water and fat to mix

Endosperm The largest portion of a kernel of grain; it is primarily starch and serves as a food supply for the sprouting seed

Energy balance The amount of energy consumed in the diet compared with the amount expended by the body over a given period

Energy-yielding nutrients Refers to carbohydrates, fats, and proteins, the nutrients that provide energy (calories) to the body

Enrichment A term used to describe the addition of nutrients to a food in order to restore those lost in processing to a level equal to or higher than that originally present

Enzymes Protein molecules that accelerate the rate of specific chemical reactions without being changed themselves

EPA   See *eicosapentaenoic acid.*

Esophagus   A portion of the gastrointestinal tract that extends from the throat to the stomach

Essential fatty acid deficiency   A condition characterized by dry, scaly skin, and poor growth that results when the diet does not supply sufficient amounts of the essential fatty acids

Essential fatty acids   Fatty acids that must be supplied in the diet because they cannot be made in the body

Essential nutrients   Nutrients that must be supplied in the diet because they cannot be made in sufficient quantities in the body to meet needs

Essential or indispensable amino acids   Amino acids that cannot be synthesized by the human body in sufficient amounts to meet needs and, therefore, must be included in the diet

Estimated Average Requirements (EARs)   Intakes recommended by the DRIs that meet the estimated nutrient needs of 50% of individuals in a gender and life-stage group

Estimated Energy Requirements (EERs)   Energy intakes recommended by the DRIs to maintain body weight

Extracellular fluid   The fluid located outside cells; it includes fluid found in the blood, lymph, gastrointestinal tract, spinal column, eyes, and joints, and that found between cells and tissues.

Fat-soluble vitamins   Vitamins that dissolve in fat; they include A, D, E, and K.

Fatty acid   An organic molecule made up of a chain of carbons linked to hydrogens with an acid group at one end

Feces   Body waste, including unabsorbed food residue, bacteria, mucus, and dead cells, which is excreted from the gastrointestinal tract by passing through the anus

Ferritin   The major iron storage protein

Fiber   Nonstarch polysaccharides in plant foods that are not broken down by human digestive enzymes

Fortification   A term used generally to describe the addition of nutrients to foods, such as the addition of vitamin D to milk

Free radical   One type of highly reactive molecule that causes oxidative damage

Fructose   A monosaccharide that is sweeter to the taste than glucose

Galactose   A monosaccharide that, along with glucose, makes up lactose

Gallbladder   An organ of the digestive system that stores bile, which is produced by the liver

Gastrointestinal tract   A hollow tube consisting of the mouth, pharynx, esophagus, stomach, small intestine, and large intestine, in which digestion and absorption of nutrients occurs

Gene   A segment of DNA that codes for a protein

Gene expression   The events of protein synthesis in which the information in a gene is used to synthesize a protein

Germ   The embryo or sprouting portion of a kernel of grain; it contains vegetable oil and vitamins.

Glucagon   A hormone made in the pancreas that stimulates the breakdown of liver glycogen and the synthesis of glucose to increase blood sugar

Gluconeogenesis   The synthesis of glucose from simple noncarbohydrate molecules; amino acids from protein are the primary source of carbons for glucose synthesis.

Glucose   A monosaccharide that is the primary carbohydrate form used to provide energy in the body; it is the sugar referred to as blood sugar.

Glycogen   A carbohydrate made of many glucose molecules linked together in a highly branched structure; it is the storage form of carbohydrates in animals.

Glycolysis   A metabolic pathway in the cytoplasm of the cell that splits glucose into two 3-carbon pyruvate molecules; the energy released from a molecule of glucose is used to make 2 ATP molecules.

Goiter   An enlargement of the thyroid gland caused by a deficiency of iodine

Heme iron   A readily absorbed form of iron found in animal products that is chemically associated with proteins such as hemoglobin and myoglobin

Hemochromatosis   An inherited condition that results in increased iron absorption

Hemoglobin   An iron-containing protein in red blood cells that binds and transports oxygen through the bloodstream to cells

High-density lipoproteins (HDLs)   Lipoproteins that pick up cholesterol from cells and transport it to the liver so that it can be eliminated from the body; a low level of HDL increases the risk of cardiovascular disease.

Homeostasis   A physiological state in which a stable internal body environment is maintained

Homocysteine   An intermediate in the metabolism of methionine; high levels in the blood increase the risk of heart disease.

Hormones   Chemical messengers that are produced in one location, released into the blood, and then elicit responses at other locations in the body

Hydrogenated fat   Fat that has had hydrogen atoms added to it to increase the number of saturated bonds

Hydrogenation   The process whereby hydrogen atoms are added to the carbon-carbon double bonds of unsaturated fatty acids, making them more saturated

Hypercarotenemia   A condition caused by an accumulation of carotenoids in the adipose tissue, causing the skin to appear yellow-orange

Hypertension   Blood pressure that is consistently elevated to 140/90 mm of mercury or greater

Hyponatremia   An abnormally low concentration of sodium in the blood

Inorganic   Containing no carbon-hydrogen bonds

Insensible losses   Fluid losses that are not perceived by the senses, such as evaporation of water through the skin and lungs

Insoluble fiber   Fiber that, for the most part, does not dissolve in water; it includes cellulose, hemicelluloses, and lignin.

Insulin   A hormone made in the pancreas that allows the uptake of glucose by body cells and has other metabolic effects, such as stimulating the synthesis of glycogen in liver and muscle

International Unit (IU)   An outdated unit of vitamin requirements, still seen on supplement labels

Interstitial fluid   The portion of the extracellular fluid located in the spaces between cells and tissues

Intracellular fluid   The fluid located inside cells

Intrinsic factor   A protein produced in the stomach that is needed for the absorption of adequate amounts of vitamin B_{12}

Ion   An atom or group of atoms that carries a negative or a positive electrical charge

Iron deficiency anemia   A condition that occurs when the oxygen-carrying capacity of the blood is decreased because there is insufficient iron to make hemoglobin

Keratin   A hard protein that makes up hair and nails

Ketones or **ketone bodies**   Molecules formed when there is not a sufficient amount of carbohydrates to completely metabolize the acetyl-CoA produced from fat breakdown

Kilocalorie   A unit of heat that is used to express the amount of energy provided by foods

Kilojoule   A measure of work that can be used to express energy intake and energy output; 4.18 kjoules = 1 kcalorie

Kwashiorkor   A form of protein-energy malnutrition in which protein is deficient; it is most common in young children who are unable to meet their high protein needs with their available diet

Lactic acid   An acid produced from pyruvate in the absence of oxygen; it is associated with fatigue during exercise.

Lactose   The disaccharide comprised of glucose and galactose; it is the sugar found in milk and other dairy products.

Lactose intolerance   The inability to digest lactose because of a deficiency of the enzyme lactase; the condition causes symptoms including intestinal gas and bloating after dairy products are consumed.

LDLs   See *low-density lipoproteins.*

Lecithin   A phospholipid that is a major component of cell membranes and is used as an emulsifier in foods

Limiting amino acid   The amino acid in shortest supply in relation to the body's need for it.

Linoleic acid   The major omega-6 fatty acid in the American diet; it is plentiful in vegetable oils

Lipases   Fat-digesting enzymes

Lipid   A group of organic molecules, most of which do not dissolve in water; they include fatty acids, glycerides, phospholipids, and sterols.

Lipid bilayer   Two layers of phospholipid molecules oriented so that the fat-soluble fatty acid tails are sandwiched between the water-soluble phosphate-containing heads

Lipoproteins   Particles containing a core of lipids surrounded by a shell of protein and phospholipid that transport lipids in blood and lymph

Low-density lipoproteins (LDLs)   Lipoproteins that transport cholesterol to cells. Elevated LDL cholesterol increases the risk of cardiovascular disease

Lutein   A carotenoid that is important in vision but cannot be converted to vitamin A

Lycopene   A carotenoid that gives tomatoes their red color but cannot be converted to vitamin A

Lymph   A clear yellowish fluid that is derived from the tissues of the body and conveyed to the bloodstream by the lymphatic vessels

Macrocytic or megaloblastic anemia   A condition in which there are abnormally large immature and mature red blood cells and a reduction in the total number of red blood cells

Macronutrients   Nutrients needed by the body in large amounts; these include water and the energy-yielding nutrients carbohydrates, lipids, and proteins.

Major minerals   Minerals needed in the diet in amounts greater than 100 mg per day or present in the body in amounts greater than 0.01% of body weight

Malabsorption   Poor absorption of nutrients in the gastrointestinal tract

Malnutrition   Any condition resulting from an energy or nutrient intake either above or below that which is optimal

Maltose   A disaccharide consisting of two molecules of glucose

Marasmus   A form of protein-energy malnutrition in which a deficiency of energy in the diet causes severe body wasting

Metabolism   The sum of all the chemical reactions that take place in a living organism

Micelles   Small particles formed in the small intestine when the products of fat digestion are surrounded by bile acids; they facilitate the absorption of fat.

Micronutrients   Nutrients needed by the body in small amounts; these include vitamins and minerals.

Mitochondria   The cellular organelles responsible for generating energy in the form of ATP for cellular activities

Molecules   Units of two or more atoms of the same or different elements bonded together

Monosaccharide   A single sugar molecule, such as glucose

Monounsaturated fatty acid (MUFA)   A fatty acid that contains one carbon-carbon double bond

Mucus   A viscous fluid secreted by glands in the gastrointestinal tract and other parts of the body; it acts to lubricate, moisten, and protect cells from harsh environments.

MUFA See *monounsaturated fatty acid.*

Myocardial infarction   Blockage of blood flow to the heart muscle causing the death of heart cells; also known as a heart attack

Myoglobin   An iron-containing protein in muscle cells

Neural tube defects   Abnormalities in the brain or spinal cord that result from errors that occur during prenatal development

Neurotransmitter   A chemical substance produced by a nerve cell that can stimulate or inhibit another cell

Non-heme iron   A poorly absorbed form of iron found in both plant and animal foods that is not part of the iron complex found in hemoglobin and myoglobin

Nutrient density   A measure of the nutrients provided by a food relative to the energy it contains

Nutrients   Chemical substances in foods that provide energy, structure, and regulation for body processes

Nutrition   A science that studies the interactions that occur between living organisms and food

Obese   Carrying excess body fat, defined as a BMI of ≥ 30 kg/m^2

Obesity   The condition of being obese

Oligosaccharides   Short-chain carbohydrates containing 3 to 10 sugar units.

Omega-3 fatty acid   A fatty acid containing a carbon-carbon double bond between the third and fourth carbons from the omega end

Omega-6 fatty acid   A fatty acid containing a carbon-carbon double bond between the sixth and seventh carbons from the omega end

Organic   Molecules that contain carbon-hydrogen bonds

Osmosis   The passive movement of water across a membrane to equalize the concentration of dissolved solutes on both sides

Osteomalacia   A vitamin D deficiency disease in adults characterized by loss of minerals from the bone matrix; it causes weak bones and increases the likelihood of bone fractures.

Osteoporosis   A bone disorder characterized by a reduction in bone mass, increased bone fragility, and an increased risk of fractures

Overnutrition   Poor nutritional status resulting from a dietary intake in excess of that which is optimal for health

Overweight   An excess of body fat, defined as a BMI ≥ 25 kg/m^2

Oxalates   Organic acids found in spinach, rhubarb, and other leafy green vegetables that can bind certain minerals and decrease their absorption

Oxidative damage   Damage caused by highly reactive oxygen molecules that steal electrons from other compounds, causing changes in structure and function

Pancreas   An organ that secretes digestive enzymes and bicarbonate ions into the small intestine during digestion

Parathyroid hormone (PTH)   A hormone secreted by the parathyroid gland that increases blood calcium levels

Peak bone mass   The maximum bone density attained at any time in life, usually occurring in young adulthood

Pellagra The disease resulting from a deficiency of niacin

Pepsin A protein-digesting enzyme produced by the stomach; it is secreted in the gastric juice in an inactive form and activated by acid in the stomach

Peptide bonds Chemical bonds between amino acids in protein

Peristalsis Coordinated muscular contractions that move food through the gastrointestinal tract

Phenylketonuria An inherited disease resulting in faulty metabolism of phenylalanine, and characterized by phenylketones in the urine; if untreated, it causes mental deficiency.

Phospholipid A type of fat that contains a phosphorus-containing group in addition to two fatty acids attached to a molecule of glycerol

Phytate An inorganic phosphorus storage compound found in seeds and grains that can bind minerals and decrease their absorption

Phytochemical A substance found in plant foods that is not an essential nutrient but may have health-promoting properties

Plaque A cholesterol-rich material that is deposited in the arterial walls of individuals with atherosclerosis

Plasma The liquid part of blood that remains when the blood cells are removed

Polypeptide A chain of amino acids

Polysaccharides Carbohydrates made up of many sugar units linked together

Polyunsaturated fatty acid (PUFA) A fatty acid that contains two or more carbon-carbon double bonds

Prebiotics Substances that pass undigested into the colon and stimulate the growth and/or activity of certain types of bacteria

Probiotics Products that contain live bacteria, which when consumed live temporarily in the colon and confer health benefits on the host

Protein complementation Combining proteins from different sources so that they collectively provide the proportions of amino acids required to meet needs

Protein quality A measure of how efficiently a protein in the diet can be used to make body proteins

Protein-energy malnutrition (PEM) A condition characterized by wasting and an increased susceptibility to infection that results from the long-term consumption of insufficient energy and protein to meet needs

PUFA See *polyunsturated fatty acid.*

Pyridoxine The chemical term for vitamin B_6

Pyruvate A 3-carbon molecule produced during the breakdown of glucose in glycolysis

Recommended Dietary Allowances (RDAs) Intakes recommended by the DRIs that are sufficient to meet the nutrient needs of almost all healthy people in a specific life-stage and gender group

Refined Refers to foods that have undergone processes that change or remove various components of the original food

Renin An enzyme produced by the kidney that aids in the conversion of angiotensin to its active form, angiotensin II

Retinoids The chemical forms of preformed vitamin A: retinol, retinal, and retinoic acid

Rhodopsin A light-sensitive compound found in the retina of the eye that is composed of the protein opsin loosely bound to retinal

Rickets A vitamin D deficiency disease in children that is characterized by poor bone development because of inadequate calcium deposition

Saliva A watery fluid produced and secreted into the mouth by the salivary glands; it contains lubricants, enzymes, and other substances

Saturated fat Fats containing fatty acids that contain no carbon-carbon double bonds

Scurvy A vitamin C deficiency disease

Simple carbohydrates Carbohydrates known as sugars that include monosaccharides and disaccharides

Soluble fiber Fiber that either dissolves when placed in water or absorbs water; it includes pectins, gums, and some hemicelluloses

Solutes Dissolved substances

Solvent A fluid in which one or more substances dissolve

Starch   A carbohydrate made of many glucose molecules linked in straight or branching chains; the bonds that hold the glucose molecules together can be broken by the human digestive enzymes.

Starvation   The most extreme form of malnutrition, resulting from a serious, or total, lack of nutrients needed for the maintenance of life

Sterols   A type of lipid with a ring structure; cholesterol is the best known sterol.

Sucrose   A disaccharide formed by linking glucose to fructose; known as table sugar, it is refined from sugar cane or sugar beets and is the only sweetener that can be called "sugar" in the ingredient list on food labels in the United States.

Sugar   The basic unit of carbohydrate; only sucrose can be called "sugar" in the ingredient list on food labels.

Tannins   Substances found in tea and some grains that can bind certain minerals and decrease their absorption

Tocopherol   The chemical name for vitamin E

Tolerable Upper Intake Level (UL)   The maximum daily intake that is unlikely to pose risks of adverse health effects to almost all individuals in the specified life-stage and gender group

Trace elements   Minerals required in the diet in amounts of 100 mg or less per day or present in the body in amounts of 0.01% of body weight or less

Trans fatty acid   An unsaturated fatty acid in which the hydrogens are on opposite sides of the double bond

Transferrin   An iron transport protein in the blood

Transit time   The amount of time it takes food and waste products to move through the gastrointestinal tract

Triglyceride   The major form of lipid in food and in the body; it consists of three fatty acids attached to a glycerol molecule

Tropical oils   The saturated plant oils (coconut, palm, and palm kernel oil) that are derived from plants grown in tropical regions

Unsaturated fat   A fatty acid that contains one or more carbon-carbon double bonds

Urea   A nitrogen-containing waste product that is excreted in the urine

Vegan   Refers to a pattern of food intake that eliminates all animal products

Veins   Vessels that carry blood toward the heart

Very-low-density lipoproteins (VLDLs)   Lipoproteins assembled by the liver that carry lipids from the liver and deliver triglycerides to body cells

Vitamins   Organic compounds needed in the diet in small amounts to promote and regulate the chemical reactions and processes needed for growth, reproduction, and maintenance of health

Warfarin   A chemical that inhibits blood clotting; it is used as both rat poison and medicine

Water intoxication   A condition that occurs when a person drinks enough water to significantly lower the concentration of sodium in the blood

Water-soluble vitamins   Vitamins that dissolve in water

Xerophthalmia   A spectrum of eye conditions resulting from vitamin A deficiency that may lead to blindness; an early symptom is night blindness, and as the deficiency continues, a lack of mucus leaves the eye dry and vulnerable to cracking and infection.

Zeaxanthin   A carotenoid found in corn and green peppers that has no vitamin A activity but provides some protection against macular degeneration

BIBLIOGRAPHY

American Cancer Society. "American Cancer Society Guidelines on Nutrition and Physical Activity for Cancer Prevention: Reducing the Risk of Cancer With Healthy Food Choices and Physical Activity." *CA: A Cancer Journal for Clinicians* 56 (2006): 254–281.

American Dental Association. "Fluoride and Fluoridation: Fluoridation Facts." Available online at http://www.ada.org/sections/professional resources/pdfs/fluoridation_facts.pdf. Accessed March 5, 2010.

American Dietetic Association. "Position of the American Dietetic Association: Weight Management." *Journal of the American Dietetic Association* 109 (2009): 330–346.

American Dietetic Association. "Position of the American Dietetic Association: Vegetarian Diets." *Journal of the American Dietetic Association* 109 (2009): 1266–1282. Available online at http://www.eatright.org/About/Content.aspx?id=8357. Accessed March 5, 2010.

Beck, M.A., O. Levander, and J. Handy. "Selenium Deficiency and Viral Infection." *Journal of Nutrition* 133 (2003): 1463S–1467S.

Burkitt, D.P., A.R.P. Walker, and N.S. Painter. "Dietary Fiber and Disease." *Journal of the American Medical Association* 229 (1974): 1068–1074.

Centers for Disease Control and Prevention. "Diabetes Fact Sheet: General information and national estimates on diabetes in the United States, 2007." Available online at http://www.cdc.gov/diabetes/pubs/factsheet07.htm. Accessed September 12, 2009.

Centers for Disease Control and Prevention. "Iron Overload and Hemochromatosis: Hereditary Hemochromatosis, 2005." Available online at http://www.cdc.gov/ncbddd/hemochromatosis/. Accessed March 5, 2010.

Centers for Disease Control and Prevention. "Obesity and Overweight, Health Consequences, 2005." Available online at http://www.cdc.gov/obesity/causes/health.html. Accessed September 12, 2009.

Centers for Disease Control and Prevention. "Physical Activity and Health: A Report of the Surgeon General." Available online at http://www.cdc.gov/nccdphp/sgr/adults.htm. Accessed March 5, 2010.

Centers for Disease Control and Prevention. "Prevalence of Overweight and Obesity Among Adults: United States 1999–2002." Available online at http://www.cdc.gov/nchs/data/hestat/obese/obese99.htm. Accessed October 12, 2009.

Centers for Disease Control and Prevention. "Spina Bifida and Anencephaly Before and After Folic Acid Mandate: United States, 1995–1996 and 1999–2000." *Morbidity and Mortality Weekly Report* 17 (2004): 362–365. Available online at http://www.cdc.gov/MMWR/preview/mmwrhtml/mm5317a3.htm. Accessed March 5, 2010.

Centers for Disease Control and Prevention. "Trends in Intake of Energy and Macronutrients–United States, 1971–2000." *Morbidity and Mortality Weekly Report* 53 (2004): 80–82.

De Wals, P., F. Tiarou, M.I. Van Allen, et al. "Reduction in Neural-Tube Defects After Folic Acid Fortification In Canada." *New England Journal of Medicine* 357 (2007): 135–142.

Eijkman, C. "Beriberi and Vitamin B1." Available online at http://nobelprize.org/educational_games/medicine/vitamin_b1/eijkman.html Accessed March 5, 2010.

Fleith M. and M.T. Clandinin. "Dietary PUFA for Preterm and Term Infants: Review Of Clinical Studies." *Critical Reviews in Food Science and Nutrition* 45(3) (2005) :205–229.

Gallagher, D., S. Heymsfield, M. Heo, et al. "Healthy Percentage Body Fat Ranges: An Approach For Developing Guidelines Based On Body Mass Index." *American Journal Clinical Nutrition* 72 (2000): 694–701.

Garland, C.F., E.D. Gorham, et al. "The Role of Vitamin D in Cancer Prevention." *American Journal of Public Health* 96 (2006): 252–261.

Gill, H. and J. Prasad. "Probiotics, Immunomodulation, and Health Benefits." *Advances in Experimental Medicine Biology* 606 (2008): 423–454.

Hemilä, H. "Vitamin C Supplementation and Common Cold Symptoms: Factors Affecting the Magnitude of the Benefit." *Medical Hypotheses* 52 (1999): 171–178.

Hill, J.O., H.R. Wyatt, G.W. Reed, and J.C. Peters. "Obesity and the Environment: Where Do We Go from Here?" *Science* 299 (2003): 853–855.

Holick, M.F. and T.C. Chen. "Vitamin D Deficiency: A Worldwide Problem with Health Consequences." *American Journal of Clinical Nutrition* 87, Suppl. (2008): 1080S–1086S.

Institute of Medicine. Food and Nutrition Board. *Dietary Reference Intakes: Calcium, Phosphorus, Magnesium, Vitamin D, and Fluoride.* Washington, D.C.: National Academies Press, 1997.

———. *Dietary Reference Intakes for Energy, Carbohydrates, Fiber, Fat, Protein and Amino Acids.* Washington, D.C.: National Academies Press, 2002.

———. *Dietary Reference Intakes for Thiamin, Riboflavin, Niacin, Vitamin B-6, Folate, Vitamin B-12, Pantothenic Acid, Biotin, and Choline.* Washington, D.C.: National Academies Press, 1998.

———. *Dietary Reference Intakes: Vitamin A, Vitamin K, Arsenic, Boron, Chromium, Copper, Iodine, Iron, Manganese, Molybdenum, Nickel, Silicon, Vanadium, and Zinc.* Washington, D.C.: National Academies Press, 2001.

———. *Dietary Reference Intakes for Vitamin C, Vitamin E, Selenium, and Carotenoids.* Washington, D.C.: National Academies Press, 2000.

———. *Dietary Reference Intakes for Water, Potassium, Sodium, Chloride, and Sulfate.* Washington, D.C.: National Academies Press, 2004.

News of the Odd. "John Harvey Kellogg Serves Corn Flakes at the San (March 7, 1897)." Available online at http://www.newsoftheodd.com/article1016.html. Accessed January 21, 2001.

Rodriguez, N.R., N.M. DiMarco, and S. Langley. "Position of the American Dietetic Association, Dietitians of Canada, and the American

College Of Sports Medicine: Nutrition And Athletic Performance." *Journal of American Dietetic Association* 109 (2009): 509–527.

Saremi, A. and R. Arora. "Vitamin E and Cardiovascular Disease." *American Journal of Therapeutic Nutrition* 2009 May 15. [E-pub ahead of print]

Shen, H.P. "Body Fluids and Water Balance." In Stipanuk, M.H. *Biochemical, Physiological, and Molecular Aspects of Human Nutrition*, 2nd ed. St. Louis: Saunders Elsevier, 2006: 973–1,000.

Steinfeld, H., P. Gerger, T. Wassenaar, et al. *Livestock's Long Shadow: Environmental Issues and Opinions, 2006*. Available online at http://www.fao.org/docrep/010/a0701e/a0701e00.HTM. Accessed March 5, 2010.

Streppel M.T., M.C. Ocké, H.C. Boshuizen, et al. "Dietary Fiber Intake in Relation to Coronary Heart Disease and All-Cause Mortality Over 40 Y: The Zutphen Study." *American Journal of Clinical Nutrition* 88 (2008): 1119–25.

U.S. Department of Health and Human Services. *Be Active Your Way: A Guide for Adults*. Office of Disease Prevention and Health Promotion U.S., 2008.

U.S. Department of Health and Human Services. *A Healthier You: Based on the Dietary Guidelines for Americans*. Office of Disease Prevention and Health Promotion U.S., 2005.

U.S. Department of Health and Human Services. *2008 Physical Activity Guidelines for Americans*. Washington, D.C.: Department of Health and Human Services, 2008.

Vieth, R. "Vitamin D Toxicity, Policy, and Science." *Journal of Bone and Mineral Research* 22, Suppl. 2 (2007): V64–V68.

World Health Organization. *Micronutrient Deficiencies: Iodine Deficiency Disorders*. Available online at http://www.who.int/nutrition/topics/idd/en/index.html. Accessed May 20, 2008.

World Health Organization. *Micronutrient Deficiencies. Vitamin A Deficiency: The Challenge*. Available online at http://www.who.int/nutrition/topics/vad/en/index.html. Accessed April 23, 2008.

World Health Organization. *Obesity and Overweight, September 2006. Fact sheet no. 311.* Available online at http://www.who.int/media centre/factsheets/fs311/en/print.html. Accessed July 2, 2009.

Young, L.R. and M. Nestle. "The Contribution of Expanding Portion Sizes to the Obesity Epidemic." *American Journal of Public Health* 92 (2002): 246–249.

FURTHER RESOURCES

Dunford, Marie. *Sports Nutrition: A Practice Manual for Professionals.* New York: American Dietetic Association, 2006.

Duyff, Roberta. *American Dietetic Association Complete Food and Nutrition Guide.* 3rd ed. John Wiley & Sons, Hoboken, NJ, 2008.

Kennedy, Eileen, ed. "Tufts University Health & Nutrition Letter." Available online http://www.tuftshealthletter.com/SampleIssue.aspx

NIH Office of Dietary Supplements. "Dietary Supplement Fact Sheets." Available online at http://ods.od.nih.gov/Health_Information/Information_About_Individual_Dietary_Supplements.aspx

Sarubin-Fragakis, Allison, American Dietetic Association. *The Health Professional's Guide to Popular Dietary Supplements*, 3rd ed. John Wiley and Sons, Hoboken, NJ, 2007.

Web Sites
American Dietetic Association
http://www.EatRight.org
This is the official Web site of the American Dietetic Association. It provides the latest guidelines and recommendations in all areas of nutrition. It also includes information about how to choose foods to keep your diet healthy.

HealthFinder.gov
http://www.healthfinder.gov/
This site provides a guide to reliable information on physical activity and other health issues.

President's Council on Physical Fitness and Sports
http://www.fitness.gov
This site provides the latest guidelines for physical fitness for Americans. It also includes information on how you can start a physical activity program today and stay active and fit for life.

USDA National Nutrient Database for Standard Reference
http://www.nal.usda.gov/fnic/foodcomp/search/
This site allows users to look up the nutrient content of foods in an online database. It is a good resource for evaluating food chocies.

We Can!
http://www.nhlbi.nih.gov/health/public/heart/obesity/wecan/
We Can! *stands for Ways to Enhance Children's Activity & Nutrition.* We Can! *is a national education program designed for parents and caregivers to help children 8 to 13 years old stay at a healthy weight.* We Can! *offers parents and families tips and fun activities to encourage healthy eating, increase physical activity, and reduce sedentary or computer and TV time.*

PICTURE CREDITS

Page

14: © Infobase Publishing

22: © Infobase Publishing

27: USDA

30: © Infobase Publishing

33: © Infobase Publishing

40: © Infobase Publishing

44: Shutterstock

49: PhotoEdit

52: © Infobase Publishing

55: © Infobase Publishing

62: © Infobase Publishing

64: © Infobase Publishing

67: © Infobase Publishing

72: © Infobase Publishing

79: © Infobase Publishing

84: © Infobase Publishing

86: AP Images

90: © Infobase Publishing

96: © Infobase Publishing

104: © Infobase Publishing

106: © Infobase Publishing

121: © Infobase Publishing

125: © Infobase Publishing

127: © Infobase Publishing

133: Landov

143: © Infobase Publishing

148: © Infobase Publishing

155: Getty Images

161: Getty Images

172: © Infobase Publishing

175: © Infobase Publishing

INDEX

Page numbers in *italics* indicate photos or illustrations; page numbers followed by *t* indicate tables.

A

absorption 13, *14*, 68–69, 82, 98–99
added refined sugar 34–36, 47
adenosine triphosphate (ATP) 13, 39, 41, 70
Adequate Intakes (AIs) 18–19
ADH. *See* antidiuretic hormone
aerobic metabolism *40*, 41
aldosterone 104–105, 144
alpha-carotene 129
alpha-linolenic acid 65
alpha-tocopherol (α-tocopherol) 135
amenorrhea 150
amino acids 17, 78–81, *79*, 82–85, *84*
anaerobic glycolysis/metabolism 39–40, *40*
anemia *121*, 121–122, 123
angiotensin II 103–104, *104*
anticoagulants 137
antidiuretic hormone (ADH) 103, *104*
antioxidants 17, 124–125, 134–135
arachidonic acid 65
ariboflavinosis 116
artificial sweeteners 46
ascorbic acid (vitamin C) 124–126, *125*
atherosclerosis 71–73, *72*
ATP. *See* adenosine triphosphate
atrophic gastritis 123–124
avidin 118

B

bacteria, intestinal 56
beriberi 112–113, 114, 115
beta-carotene (β-carotene) 126
beta-cryptoxanthin 129
bile 68

bile acids 54, *55*, 68
bioavailability 140–142
biotin 118
birth defects 120–121, 122
blood clotting 136–137
blood glucose regulation 38–39
bloodletting 156
blood pressure 68, 71, 144, 145
blood sugar 30. *See also* glucose
body mass index (BMI) 170–171
body temperature regulation 98
bone health, calcium and 147–149
bone mass, peak 149
bran 32–34, *33*
B vitamins 112. *See also names of specific vitamins, e.g.,* biotin

C

caffeine 109
calcitonin 147
calcium 131, 146–149, *148*
caloric needs 168–169*t*, 169–170
calorie, defined 11
carbohydrates 29–47
    dietary choices 174–175
    dietary requirement for 44–46
    digestion of 36–37
    functions of 38–39
    healthy vs. unhealthy 41–44, *44*
    in human diet 32–36
    metabolism of 39–41, *40*
    overview 15, 16*t*, 47
    structure of 29, *30*
    types of 29–32
    unrefined vs. refined 32, 174–175
cardiovascular disease. *See* heart disease
carotenoids 126, 129
cavities 42
cell differentiation 128
cell membranes 66, 68
cellular respiration 39–41, *40*
chemical reactions, water and 97–98

chloride 142–145
cholesterol 16, 54, *55*, 66–68, 73
chromium 162–163
chromium picolinate 162
chylomicrons 69
citric acid cycle 41
cobalamin (vitamin B$_{12}$) 122–124
coenzymes 113
cofactors 139
colds, vitamin C for 125
collagen 124, *125*
colon 51
colon cancer 55–57
colonic diverticula *52*, 53
complex carbohydrates 32, 47
copper 156–157
corn flakes 53
cretinism 162

D

Daily Value (DV) 23
DASH diet (Dietary Approaches to
    Stop Hypertension) 145
dehydration 105–106, *106*
dental caries 42
deoxyribonucleic acid (DNA) 83
DHA. *See* docosahexaenoic acid
diabetes mellitus 38–39, 43–44, *44*, 54
diarrhea 101
dicoumarol 137
diet, healthy 166–180. *See also*
    nutrition
        carbohydrate, fat, and protein
            balance in 173–177
        overview 166–167, 180
        tools for choosing 20–26
        vitamins and minerals in
            177–180
        weight maintenance and 167–
            171, 168–169*t*, *175*, 177*t*
Dietary Approaches to Stop
    Hypertension (DASH) diet 145
dietary fiber. *See* fiber, dietary
Dietary Guidelines for Americans 24
Dietary Reference Intakes (DRIs) 18–19
dietary requirements
        for carbohydrates 44–46
        for lipids 73–75, 76
    for minerals 140–142, 141*t*
    for proteins 87–88, 88*t*
    for vitamins 112, 113*t*
    for water 109–110
dietary supplements 10, 20, 56, 65,
    179–180
digestion 13, *14*, 36–37, 68–69, 82
digestive system 13, *14*, 50–51
disaccharides 31
diverticulosis *52*, 53
DNA (deoxyribonucleic acid) 83
docosahexaenoic acid (DHA) 65, 66
DRIs (Dietary Reference Intakes)
    18–19
DV (Daily Value) 23

E

EARs (Estimated Average
    Requirements) 18
EERs. *See* Estimated Energy
    Requirements
eicosanoids 68
eicosapentaenoic acid (EPA) 65, 66
electrolytes 95, 142–145, *143*
electron transport chain 41
empty calories 35
endosperm 32–34, *33*
energy balance 12
energy needs 168–169*t*, 169–170
energy sources 11–12, 38, 39–41, 68,
    70, 85
energy-yielding nutrients 11
environmental costs of livestock
    production 92
EPA. *See* eicosapentaenoic acid
essential fatty acid deficiency 66
essential nutrients 10, 65–66, 80
Estimated Average Requirements
    (EARs) 18
Estimated Energy Requirements
    (EERs) 19, 168–169*t*, 169–170
exercise
        glycogen stores and 31
        water consumption during 107,
            109
        in weight maintenance 168–169,
            171–173, 177*t*
extracellular fluid 95

F

fats. *See* lipids
fat-soluble vitamins 111–112
fatty acids 15, 60, 61, *62*, 65–66
female athletes 150
ferritin 154
fiber, dietary 15, 32, 48–59
    bioavailability of minerals and 141
    in digestive tract 36, 50–51
    health effects of *52, 52–57, 55*
    overview 58–59
    problems with 57–58
    requirements for 58
    types of 48–50, *49, 50t*
fluid balance 102–108, *104*
fluoride 163–164
fluorosis 163
folate (folic acid) 120–122, *121*
food guides 24–26
food labels 21–23, *22*, 35, 174–175
food water content 98–99, *98t*
fortification 10, 178–179
free radicals 17, 124–125
fructose 29–30
fruit sugar 30

G

galactose 29–30
gallbladder 68–69
gastrointestinal (GI) tract 13, *14*,
    50–51
gene expression 128
germ, of grain 32–34, *33*
glucagon 38, 39
gluconeogenesis 39
glucose 29–30, 31, 38–39
glycogen 31, 32
glycolysis 39
goiter 160, *161*, 162

H

HDLs. *See* high-density lipoproteins
healthy diet. *See* diet, healthy
heart disease
    fiber and 54, *55*
    lipids and 71–73, *72*
    risk factors for 74–75t
    vitamin deficiency and 120, 122

heme iron 153
hemochromatosis 155–156
hemoglobin 119, 152–153
high-density lipoproteins (HDLs) 70,
    73
high-fiber diets 51, 53, 54–58
homeostasis 12
homocysteine 120, 122
hormones 12
hydrogenated fats 63, *64*
hyperactivity 42
hypercarotenemia 130
hypertension 71, 145
hyponatremia 106–108

I

indigestible carbohydrates 36–37
infant formulas 65
insensible water losses 101
insoluble fiber 49, *50t*
insulin 38, 162
interstitial fluid 95
intestinal bacteria 56
intracellular fluid 95
intrinsic factor 123
iodine 160–162, *161*
iron 20, 152–156, *155*
iron deficiency anemia 154, *155*, 156

K

Kellogg, John Harvey 53
keratin 128
Keshan disease 159–160
ketones 43
kidneys 103–105, 144–145
kilocalories 11
kilojoules 11
kwashiorkor 85–86, *86*

L

labels. *See* food labels
lactic acid 39–40
lactose intolerance 37
LDLs. *See* low-density lipoproteins
linoleic acid 63, 65
lipases 68
lipid bilayer 66

lipids 60–77. *See also* fatty acids
    cholesterol 66–68, 73
    dietary choices 175–176
    dietary requirement for 73–75, 76
    digestion, absorption, and
        transport of 68–70
    fatty acids 60, 61, *62*, 65–66
    functions of 68
    heart disease and 71–73, *72*,
        74–75*t*
    metabolism of 70–71
    overview 15–16, 16*t*, 60, 75–77
    phospholipids 60, 66, *67*
    saturated fats 15, 61–63, 176
    sterols 60, 66–68
    triglycerides 60, 61, *62*
    unsaturated fats 15–16, 63–65,
        64, 176
lipoproteins 69–70, 73
livestock production 92
low-density lipoproteins (LDLs) 70, 73
lutein 129
lycopene 129
lymph 69

M

macrocytic anemia *121*, 121–122
macronutrients 15, 16*t*
magnesium 151–152
malabsorption 123–124
malnutrition 19
manganese 158–159
marasmus 85, *86*, 86–87
megaloblastic anemia *121*, 121–122
metabolism 13, 39–41, *40*, 70–71
micelles 69
micronutrients 15, 16*t*
minerals 139–165
    calcium 146–149, *148*
    chromium 162–163
    copper 156–157
    deficiency of, high-fiber diets
        and 56
    dietary choices 177–180
    electrolytes 142–145, *143*
    fluoride 163–164
    iodine 160–162, *161*
    iron 152–156, *155*
    magnesium 151–152

    manganese 158–159
    molybdenum 164
    overview 16*t*, 18, 139–140,
        164–165
    phosphorus 150–151
    requirements for 140–142, 141*t*
    selenium 159–160
    sulfur 152
    zinc 157–158
molybdenum 164
monosaccharides 29–30
monounsaturated fatty acid (MUFA)
    63
myocardial infarction 71
myoglobin 153
MyPyramid 24–26, *27*

N

nerve conduction 142–143, 146
neural tube defects 120–121, 122
neurotransmitters 85
niacin 116–118
non-heme iron 153
nutrient density 26
nutrients
    classes of 15–18, 16*t*
    deficiency or excess of 19–20
    digestion and absorption of 13, *14*
    essential 10
    functions of 10–12
    recommended amounts 18–19
    sources of 9–10
    utilization of 13
nutrition 9–28. *See also* nutrients
    dietary recommendation tools
        24–26, *27*
    food labels and 21–23, *22*
    optimal. *See* diet, healthy
    overview 26–28
nutritional claims 21
"Nutrition Facts" labels *22*, 23

O

obesity 19, 43
obesity epidemic 171–173, *172*, 174, *175*
oligosaccharides 36–37
omega-3 fatty acids 65, 73
omega-6 fatty acids 63–64

Oral Rehydration Solutions 101
osmosis 95–96, *96*
osteomalacia 131–132
osteoporosis 148–150
overnutrition 19
oxalates 141

P

pantothenic acid 119
parathyroid hormone (PTH) 131, 147,
 148
pellagra 116, 117
PEM. *See* protein-energy malnutrition
 (PEM)
pepsin 82
peptide bonds 80–81
pernicious anemia 123
phenylketonuria 80
phospholipids 60, 66, *67*
phosphorus 150–151
physical activity. *See* exercise
phytates 141
phytochemicals 9, 178
plaque 71
plasma 95
polar bear liver 130
polypeptides 81
polysaccharides 32
polyunsaturated fatty acid (PUFA) 63
portion size 171, *175*, 176
potassium 142–145
prebiotics 56
probiotic therapy 56
protein complementation 89–91, *90*
protein-energy malnutrition (PEM)
 85–87, *86*
proteins 78–93
  chemical structure of 78–81, *79*
  dietary choices 176–177
  dietary requirement for 87–88,
   88*t*
  digestion and absorption of 82
  functions of 81–82
  health and 85–87, *86*
  overview 16–17, 16*t*, 93
  synthesis of 83–84, *84*
  vegetarian diets and 89–93,
   89*t*, *90*

PTH. *See* parathyroid hormone
PUFA (polyunsaturated fatty acid) 63
pyridoxine (vitamin B$_6$) 119–120

R

Recommended Dietary Allowances
 (RDAs) 18–19
refined carbohydrates 32, 34–36, 47
regulatory nutrients 12
renin-angiotensin system 103–105,
 104
retinoic acid 127, 128
retinoids 126
retinol *127*, 127–128
rhodopsin *127*, 127–128
riboflavin 115–116
rickets 131–132, *133*

S

saturated fats 15, 61–63, 176
scurvy 124
selenium 159–160
serving size 171, *175*, 176
simple carbohydrates 31, 47
sodium 142–145, *143*
sodium loss. *See* hyponatremia
soluble fiber 49–50, 50*t*
solvent, water as 97–98
starches 15, 32, 37
starvation 19
sterols 60, 66–68
stool volume 51, 52–53
structural nutrients 12
sugar consumption 42
sugars 15, 34–36, 47
sugar substitutes 46
sulfur 152
supplements. *See* dietary supplements

T

tannins 141
temperature regulation 98
thiamin 112–115
thirst 102–103
thyroid hormones 160–161
tocopherol (vitamin E) 134–136

Tolerable Upper Intake Level 19
trace elements 140
trans fat 16, 63, *64*
transferrin 153–154, 156
transit time, intestinal 51
transport 68–69, 97
triglycerides 15, 60, 61, *62*
tropical oils 61

U
unsaturated fats 15–16, 63–65, *64*, 176
urine color, dehydration and 105, *106*

V
vegan diets 89
vegetarian diets 89–93, 89*t*, *90*
very-low-density lipoproteins
    (VLDLs) 69–70
vitamins 12, 16*t*, 17, 111–138
    biotin 118
    deficiency of, high-fiber diets
        and 56
    dietary choices 177–180
    folate (folic acid) 120–122, *121*
    functions of 111
    niacin 116–118
    overdosage of 20
    pantothenic acid 119
    requirements for 112, 113*t*
    riboflavin 115–116
    thiamin 112–115
    vitamin A 126–130, *127*
    vitamin B$_6$ 119–120
    vitamin B$_{12}$ 122–124
    vitamin C 124–126, *125*

vitamin D 130–134, *133*, 146
vitamin E 134–136
vitamin K 136–137
water-soluble vs. fat-soluble
    111–112
VLDLs (very-low-density
    lipoproteins) 69–70

W
warfarin 136, 137
water 94–110
    body distribution of 95–96,
        96
    dietary sources of 99–100, 99*t*
    as essential nutrient 17
    functions of 97–98
    losses of 100–102
    requirements for 109–110
water balance 102–108, *104*
water fluoridation 163, 164
water intoxication 106
water-soluble vitamins 111–112
weight maintenance 167–171,
    168–169*t*, *172*, *175*, 177*t*
Wernicke-Korsakoff syndrome 114
whole foods 178
whole grains 32–34, *33*

X
xerophthalmia 128

Z
zeaxanthin 129
zinc 157–158

ABOUT THE AUTHOR

LORI A. SMOLIN, PH.D., received her B.S. degree from Cornell University where she studied human nutrition and food science. She received her doctorate from the University of Wisconsin at Madison. Her doctoral research focused on B vitamins, homocysteine accumulation, and genetic defects in homocysteine metabolism. She completed postdoctoral training both at the Harbor-U.C.L.A. Medical Center, where she studied human obesity, and at the University of California at San Diego, where she studied genetic defects in amino acid metabolism. She has published in these areas in peer-reviewed journals. She and Mary Grosvenor are coauthors of several well-respected, college-level nutrition textbooks and are contributing authors to a middle-school text. Dr. Smolin is currently at the University of Connecticut, where she teaches in the Department of Nutritional Science. Courses she has taught include introductory nutrition, life-cycle nutrition, food preparation, nutritional biochemistry, general biochemistry, and introductory biology.

MARY B. GROSVENOR, M.S., R.D., received her B.A. degree in English from Georgetown University and her M.S. in nutrition sciences from the University of California at Davis. She is a registered dietitian (R.D.) with experience in public health, clinical nutrition, and nutrition research. She has published in peer-reviewed journals in the areas of nutrition and cancer and methods of assessing dietary intake. She and Lori Smolin are the coauthors of several well-respected, college-level nutrition textbooks and are contributing authors to a middle-school text. Grosvenor has taught introductory nutrition to community college and nursing school students. In addition to writing and teaching, she works as a hospital dietitian and certified diabetes educator who counsels patients and advises other health professionals in the area of clinical nutrition.